Tick Tock India

John Scott Gagne

ISBN: 978-1-7390809-0-7 (Paperback)

ISBN: 978-1-7390809-1-4 (E-book)

Editing by PaperTrue Ltd.

Cover art by Amelia Gagne

Book design by John Gagne

Printed in US

Published by PaperTrue

Contents

Summary

In **Tick Tock India,** John S. Gagne presents a view of outsourcing in India, with a focus on three Indian cities: Hyderabad, Bengaluru, and Chennai, and offers tools and advice to consider before outsourcing. John S. Gagne is well-experienced in the field of outsourcing, having been both a provider and a consumer.

The book explains why a company would outsource—cost reduction being the most prominent reason—and the risks and benefits associated with it in an Indian context. However, approaching a contract with an outsource vendor has its challenges, as they view it with the experience of a seasoned player in this field compared to the organization looking to outsource, which has stepped foot in this field for the first time.

The book then goes into the details of outsourcing in India. It explains the country's education level and work ethics in a social context, the infrastructure and commuting issues that might hinder the smooth operation of work, and how the composition of the outsource team affects the work. It also presents advise on how to tackle such issues and manage on-site support staff from the outsource team. Then, the details of the economic, geological, social, political, and healthcare situation in India and how it can affect outsourcing are given. These sections discuss the issues hindering India's economic growth; the geological problems and how they affect outsourcing, focusing on three cities; how India is faring in the technology space; its internal geo-political situation, and its relations with its neighbors. Reports and/or news articles back the information in this book.

Tick Tock India will be of considerable help to organizations considering outsourcing their work to an Indian outsource vendor. It will help them to understand what to expect, define the terms of the contract, and manage their outsource teams.

Introduction

The idea for this book was conceived 8 years ago, shortly after joining a high-tech firm that heavily invested in providing outsource hosting and technical support through a "follow the sun" format. This company facilitates the installation, operation, and support of software and hardware components for systems in various locations across the world. It primarily relies on resources in three urban locations in India, namely Hyderabad, Bangalore, and Chennai. There are other locations in India where outsourcing can be found but these three cities are areas that represent a large concentration of workers involved in IT services. Hence, I focused on these physical areas for potential operational disruptors.

My position in this high-tech company was as the Director of Client Services covering the Northeast of the US. That position followed my work in a leading biotech company where I managed an IT purchasing and contracting group. Shortly after being offered and accepting the purchasing and contracts manager role, I was promoted to a project group by our CIO. The company's executive team had realized that to maintain our substantial worldwide growth, a complete overhaul of our back office and manufacturing systems was required. This represented a major disruption to our internal IT, Financial, and Operational Management groups. Obviously, internally staffing up to handle this workload seemed impractical and unlikely to get the work completed in a timely fashion. We determined that to accomplish such a task, some internal team members had to be shifted across several critical roles, and that outsourcing the project through a systems integrator was our best chance at being successful for such an impactful and transformative effort. I was the primary delivery director of the vendors involved in the outsourcing including the systems integrator (Deloitte), systems operations facility (EDI), and software support team (Oracle). This represented an expected project cost of approximately $165 Million USD over a 2-year period.

Contracts were signed and the project was launched to get work started on this vast transformative project. Meanwhile, troubles in our manufacturing process derailed our progress as a company, and a questionable response from a senior executive resulted in the FDA issuing a consent decree against our company. This opened the door to a hostile takeover, and the eventual merger of our company into a larger, marginally related firm, and the cessation of all work on our project less than 24 months into the effort. These events prompted my interaction with one of our vendor companies and accepting an offer to join them. That was my entry into the world of outsourcing as a provider rather than a consumer.

This is my first time experiencing "behind the scenes" of what outsourcing really entails and the lessons, benefits, and pitfalls one should expect when entering this arena as a consumer. I hope that this book provides a few cautionary thoughts for those considering moving into this model either because it is necessary for their business or because they are already involved and seek to improve the responsiveness and effectiveness of their provider(s). The best situation would be where one considers or is about to make the leap. This book can give some guidance as to what to pay close attention to from the service provider, the terms of the agreement, and how best to manage the provider going forward.

At that point, I saw outsourcing as a sole source risk to operations much like we would assess any risk to operations and began thinking of mitigation strategies. This search lead me to this book where I asked myself "Why India?" I did not know enough about the nation to answer my own question. This put me on a path to attain a deeper understanding of the nation and the issues, risks, geology, weather, people, and geo-political realities it must deal with. Moreover, it made me realize that assessment of risk within the traditional contracting/procurement world or the professional staff within IT is typically too narrow to fully analyze the risks of outsourcing. We simply do not have a deep or wide enough view of the questions involved in making the decision. It is likely that the advice we do get comes from those who have a financial incentive to sell us on the benefits but no incentive to deeply discuss and present the risk analysis of such a decision. This does not mean that outsourcing lacks merit, good rationales, or sound business reasons, but that the decision can be reached without truly understanding the implications and sources of frustration and the disconnects that will be encountered because of making such a move. In many cases, it is the right thing to do that can help us avoid severe and potentially crippling issues to our business and desired business outcomes. It does, however, suggest that digging into the analysis of risks involved should be a separate and detailed step beyond the capabilities and experience of those around us as we contemplate the move. This book attempts to offer some tools and a wider view of that decision with no incentive other sharing what I have learned. At the very least, I hope what I have learned can give some ideas as to what to consider, as well as a few questions to ask before signing an outsourcing agreement with whichever firm one selects.

It is important that I leave a comment properly crediting the strength of India's outsourcing, consulting, and support capabilities. They are high level and can offer some of the finest technical minds available, second to none anywhere in the world. I have met and worked with some of the best owing to my interactions first as an employer and finally as a member and leader of these teams. None of the hesitations or cautions I have concerning outsourcing in India result from the lack of competence of the people involved. The people are often top level. However, the circumstances within which the nation operates must be understood and incorporated into one's decision-making process. These facts are true, and the challenges are real. One must be aware and conscious as they go through the process of assessment, gear up for how to best support the decision, and prepare oneself for what one will encounter once engaged in the process.

Several traditional risk analysis topics have been looked at and applied to this overview of India to conduct research that ensures a representation of an accurate and in-depth observation of those areas. Since all things are subject to change, my data is based on what I could validate at that specific point in time. My first caution, therefore, is to ensure that no significant changes have occurred to invalidate the data presented in this book. Since many of my sources are public, they can be updated annually. For instance, I refer to the World Health Organization's annual reports and the US' CIA World Book, which are both updated on a regular basis. Other sources may not be as easily updated, considering that they were volumes written once and published at a certain point in time. The bibliography of the various volumes and writings I have accessed and read are published at the end of this book. Other data in this book are relatively stable and unlikely to change significantly in short periods of time. For instance, geological data is a well-documented and understood condition in India, but even this can change drastically if some catastrophic event takes place. I am less concerned about those details being usurped by current events and changing. This is because such events like major earthquakes, geo-political actions including wars, border incursions, or significant economic disasters get widely reported, tend to "self-update" themselves worldwide, as well as force one to apply the new information and take on fresh evaluations.

I believe that the topics covered in this book are inclusive of the events and conditions that need to be understood and at least reviewed for stability and functional condition, as well as be monitored on a regular basis to ensure the security and reliability of the investment.

However, I am sure one knows that risk analysis is not a onetime action item: it is a defined moment in time that will be subject to change. In many cases, some items on the list may remain somewhat static and continue as such for some period. In other cases, the risk factors are subject to swift and catastrophic changes at any given moment. An understanding of what is likely to happen versus what is expected to happen is important to be updated and current in the periodic reviews of the status of risks. Depending on how the organization is structured for managing the outsource investment, a member of the team should be responsible for maintaining a current review of the risks and where they stand on a regular basis. Any event that could leave the system as a "smoking hole in the ground" should be monitored on a regular basis. Those events that could happen versus those that might happen should set the priorities on what and how often one monitors and reports the environment around their systems. My example is simple, if I am in San Francisco, California, I would want to monitor earthquake conditions more often than if I am in Hartford, Connecticut. Not that Hartford is immune to earthquakes, but that it is certainly less likely than San Francisco for a significant earthquake event. Hence, checking on US Geological Earthquake Data could be a routine and regular task if one's systems are in one zone versus the other:

India Seismology Tracking Center: https://riseq.seismo.gov.in/riseq/earthquake

List of Risks to Monitor in This Book:

1. Work Force
    a. Stability
    b. Competence
2. Economic Stability of the nation
3. Geological Risks
4. Technological Improvements
5. Geo-political Instability
6. Health Care Issues
7. Social Upheaval
8. Civil Structure Instability
    a. Power and Energy Stability
    b. Domestic Transport and International Accessibility – Intermodal
    c. Health Systems
    d. Educational Systems
    e. Water/Sanitation
    f. Environmental Compliance
    g. Political Stability
    h. Public Safety and Security Stability
    i. Interconnectivity
        I. Banking (BIC/SWIFT)
            a. https://bicswift.org
        II. Intercontinental cable connectivity
            a. https://www.submarinecablemap.com

Chapter 1

Why are you outsourcing and the Organizational Risks

Simple Realities

The *"Deloitte Global Report of Outsourcing 2020"* as well as the reason most cited for outsourcing, indicate cost as 70% of why a company outsources with other reasons lagging far behind this principal driver. The battle for a large-scale outsourcing effort will be an internal one. Yes, there will be risks and difficulties putting so many of one's eggs in a single vendor's basket, should one fully implement such an operational scheme. However, these external challenges will be simple compared to the internal challenges. These issues can be mitigated with clear and concise messaging and explanation of the rationales behind the decision. One must start by having a few concepts that are carefully understood and widely known before the project gets underway. Why does one outsource? Can this be defined and explained in a few sentences? What happens if one does not outsource? What is its impact on the team? What are the training/retraining plans to deal with the new systems? Who among the executive levels will be impacted by the reporting and accounting systems and how will it impact their revenue arrangements? Do you have their buy-in? What about the repatriation of revenue and funding impacts? Are these clearly understood from one's finance and treasury operations? If there have been revenue flexibilities in reporting prior to the adoption of new systems, will these be exposed? If so, who will that impact?

Ultimately, if the rationale is cost reduction driving a continued expansion of outsourcing, then the economics will eventually catch up sufficiently and begin to erode the value of this outcome. For instance, the cost of land and property in Hyderabad is already beginning to escalate dramatically. There is a very good assessment of pricing pressures at a site called Asset Monkey, which breaks down a city like Hyderabad into its neighborhood/industrial areas (https://assetmonk.com/land-rates-in-hyderabad/). A recent article in **The Hindu Times of India** has quoted the following increase in land values in a major urban center: prices of land in New Delhi have noticed an increase of 17.01%, which is 6.23% more than the last year; Mumbai experienced an increase of 8.84%; and Pune registered highest annual price of 33.33%. Obviously, the per acre costs are not on par with the mega urban centers of the west or east, but it is on the move, and this impacts the equation for cost considerations. The same escalation is evident in India's infrastructure projects of buildings, highways, bridges, etc. The extent and time when such a change in cost structure significantly tips the scale against making a commitment to outsource in a particular area is only a matter of time. The irony of this statement is that a disaster event can immediately upset the entire equation and tip the scale dramatically, so the cost equation is simply a matter of time in those terms. Further, I summarize that cost as a decision basis is a double-edged sword. It is true that we get what we pay for, not all bargains are the benefit we hope for, and, certainly, there are "over the horizon" costs that are inherent in a bargain's DNA.

The decision to outsource has the benefit of reducing multiple costs only if it also shifts the cost of mitigation and contingencies to some third party and out of the hands of the corporate entity. Outsourcing theoretically amortizes the cost of creating and maintaining those strategies from a single user across multiple users with the supposed benefit of reducing the cost for all users simultaneously. Unfortunately, it does not shift the responsibility for any failures because of a risk event impacting the business. It may give some level of recourse in terms of financial recovery or exposure, but the responsibility cannot be shifted. All the responsibilities of the usual risks can be documented and covered under an agreement with the outsourcing vendor from simple power outages, data loss, and interconnectivity issues to labor disputes up to and including the "smoking hole in the ground" scenario; however, the ultimate responsibility remains with the entity who owns and manages the business. The knowledge that some level of financial recovery is possible due to some risk event is an attractive thought to an entity that runs a large IT organization and supports whatever business sits atop that infrastructure. The fact, however, is that outsource vendors are highly sensitive to these financial exposures, such that they protect themselves very well within the terms of their agreements and will not give up exposure control even in very difficult and detailed negotiations. As competitive as the push for cloud-based, demand based, or on-site solutions maybe, the legal teams behind the organizations selling these services maintain a vice like grip on exactly what they will and will not agree to from financial recovery terms and disaster recovery terms in the RTO/RPO agreements they will negotiate. Be prepared to walk away because they will. When you calculate the cost benefits, be sure to include a very detailed look at the cost versus recovery that you will receive in the event of a risk. It may reduce the benefit substantially. If you have three good suits in your luggage and some jewelry, and the airline loses the bag, what good is a $250 check for your inconvenience?

The current day business philosophy uses terms like "focusing on the core business," which has replaced the 30-year-old business philosophy of "vertical integration" where we owned and operated all processes that had an input and impact on the business. This philosophy at the time was precisely aimed at controlling the inputs to our business, which could impact the product we produced. It was a philosophy to mitigate risks. As an example, I worked for a firm that made flash bulbs for cameras; light bulbs were also one of their products. The extent of their vertical integration included owning the lead mines and the glass and metal fabrication firms that were components of their final product. In another example, I worked on a project in North Africa where the idea of vertical integration was "on steroids", building a one million square foot, single level manufacturing plant that was 98% vertically integrated to the point of mixing their own ferrite compounds for the antenna components of the electronic devices they intended to produce. So much for offloading non-core business activities. How trends change.

Every outsource user is competing for and feeding on the same diet of application skills, database management, security management, and development skill sets. The ship is on a sea experiencing the exact same weather conditions as every other outsourcer. The best bet for weathering these storms is to be as precise and detailed as possible when setting sail. Give oneself time to negotiate and document by contract in as much detail as possible.

Hopefully, some of the ideas and data presented in this book will trigger your team to think about and codify as many of these potential risks as possible as you define the agreement between your company and the selected outsource vendor. Negotiate carefully and be as detailed as possible in the resulting agreement. Stated later in this book is this fact your selected outsource vendor has been down this road multiple times, while you will likely only do this once or twice. Be sure your team has some very experienced members as part of the negotiation team and give them the latitude and time they need to fully explore and work out the agreement details.

While many will say that the contract is simply the divorce papers in case things go badly otherwise the document will sit in a drawer and go dormant, I will disagree and say that far from a "just in case" pre-nuptial agreement, the document is the foundation of your relationship, expectations, decisions, and metrics holding your two entities on the same path forward and within the agreed upon boundaries and guideposts. The outsource vendor will want as much flexibility as possible for as good a margin as they can get, and you will want specific outcomes and results at a cost that is reasonable and that allows you to conduct your business successfully with as little disruption as possible.

List the stakeholders in the negotiation team. If you are an international organization, be careful not to let the project be defined as Euro-centric or US centric, etc. This will setup the conditions for disinterest, sabotage, or otherwise immediately establish barriers. Keeping the view of the project as being inclusive and widely beneficial to all segments and sections of the company is not an easy task, so engage the key stakeholders representing these areas early and quickly. Who are they and are the pros and cons to the entire idea of outsourcing? Be sure that the skeptics are included for two reasons, namely they may bring up good ideas, objections, and concerns that the pro team have overlooked and getting their participation up-front will help dispel sniping from the sidelines later. Here, I am assuming that the budget and commitment for this extensive effort has the support from the senior management team up to and including the board if required. There can be no doubt that such a significant project is a major upheaval in your company impacting the systems, people, funds, processes, and reporting.

My task in this book was then to dig into the technique and areas of what we measure and think about and test when considering the risks. The ideas are universal, but my focus is on India and the challenges I have discovered and learned because of my direct experiences as a provider and client. As I learned more about the operations of these resources and the realities of how we rationalize risk, I began to learn more about the single source and what the risks were of putting so many eggs into one basket. We are operating in a silo by considering, analyzing, and making assumptions about our one system when in fact we are literally side by side with dozens of other systems and operating within a shared team under the same roof as the company down the street from us or dozens of others across our nation and multiple national borders. How do we factor that idea in our risk analysis? Do we think that if our ship survives the storm but dozens of others' do not, we will somehow be fine? How broadly do we think? How much of the world is coalescing around a sole source? Did we consider the integrated nature of the supply chain in our analysis? I may be able to buy product from company A in China and get it shipped to the west coast of the US, but if there is no one to meet the ship and off load the cargo or drive the cargo to my loading dock in Boston, what happens to my business?

Your key input to the outsourcer is going to be the data you provide: Daily transactions, revenue and forecasting, HR, Operations, Manufacturing, Tax, Treasury, Payroll, Lab Results, Development, Engineering, etc. Every aspect becomes a data stream that feeds into your system. Decide up front if this will be a multiple or single database. Determine how that data is going to be transmitted from each of these operations to that data base(s). My experience was that a single data base was the most manageable and practical. One will need to research and make the decision on how to consolidate your data, secure it, back it up, and gather valuable reporting from it. Your network team will need to determine the kind and capacity of data connections to run. I will advise to make those connections a redundant system. The entire outsource depends on getting that data in a secure, timely, and consistent manner. Calculating the capacity is not a simple task so close attention will be needed to get that right in the very beginning. Your local telecom business will be an important part of that discussion. Understand your options because the provider will have a menu of options based on the size of the "pipe" you select all at some cost. Calculate the need based on your typical business cycles including the heavy periods of month end/quarterly reporting and product introduction periods.

On the processing side of the system(s), you will be offered deals based on the automatic capacity flexibility that can scale up and down depending on the demand. Ensure that you know your averages over the course of your annual run rates for some reasonable period and understand that there will be one or two extraordinary demands here and there just because it always happens. The calculations to find a realistic "headroom" being allowed is a wise method here. To delay month end closing because the pipe is too small is something you can avoid completely with a smart calculation process and not being overly fixated on the cost of redundant telephone lines. There is no value in those savings when the CFO calls to say that closing is delayed for a week because of data availability.

Chapter 2

Skills and Challenges of Your Workforce

Who are Indians?

A quick overview of the people who populate India today.

The Indus Valley civilization, one of the world's oldest, flourished during the 3rd and 2nd centuries BCE and extended into northwestern India. Aryan tribes from the northwest infiltrated the Indian subcontinent about 1500 BCE; their merger with the earlier Dravidian inhabitants created the classical Indian culture. The Maurya Empire of the 4th and 3rd centuries BCE - which reached its zenith under ASHOKA - united much of South Asia. The Golden Age ushered in by the Gupta dynasty (4th to 6th centuries AD) saw a flowering of Indian science, art, and culture. Islam spread across the subcontinent over a period of 700 years. In the 10th and 11th centuries, Turks and Afghans invaded India and established the Delhi Sultanate. In the early 16th century, the emperor BABUR established the Mughal Dynasty, which ruled India for more than three centuries. European explorers began establishing footholds in India during the 16th century.

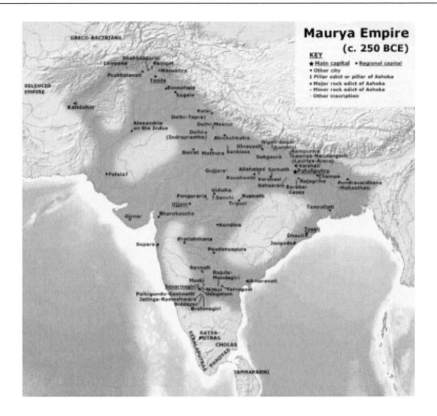

By the 19th century, Great Britain had become the dominant political power on the subcontinent and India was seen as the "Jewel in the Crown" of the British Empire. The British Indian Army played a vital role in both World Wars. Years of nonviolent resistance to British rule, led by Mohandas GANDHI and Jawaharlal NEHRU, eventually resulted in Indian independence in 1947. Large-scale communal violence took place before and after the subcontinent partition into two separate states - India and Pakistan. The neighboring countries have fought three wars since independence, the last of which was in 1971 and resulted in East Pakistan becoming the separate nation of Bangladesh. India's nuclear weapons tests in 1998 emboldened Pakistan to conduct its own tests that same year. In November 2008, terrorists originating from Pakistan conducted a series of coordinated attacks in

Mumbai, India's financial capital. India's economic growth following the launch of economic reforms in 1991, a massive youthful population, and a strategic geographic location have contributed to India's emergence as a regional and global power. However, India still faces pressing problems such as environmental degradation, extensive poverty, and widespread corruption, and its restrictive business climate challenges economic growth expectations.

India is the world's second largest population second to China in terms of the number of people. To put this into perspective and get an understanding of the enormity of the difficulty in providing a sustainable infrastructure, here are some comparisons of the populations of other nations in the world and their relative land masses.

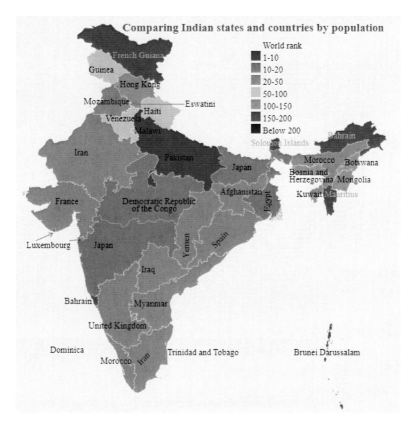

In addition to the raw volume of people, it is important to understand the current demographic by age range since these are the impacting numbers of your work force. Moreover, they represent the generations that are most likely to require long-term employment, income, consumer goods, and services of an expanding economic impact on the nation requiring health care, goods and services, and basic infrastructure like water, power and sanitation, waste management, recycling, etc. These are detailed later in this book with spreadsheets populated and categorized to these specific areas.

According to CIA Factbook, the current population demographic by age is as follows[3]:

0-14 years: 26.31% (male 185,017,089/female 163,844,572)

15-24 years: 17.51% (male 123,423,531/female 108,739,780)

25-54 years: 41.56% (male 285,275,667/female 265,842,319)

55-64 years: 7.91% (male 52,444,817/female 52,447,038)

65 years and over: 6.72% (2020 Est.) (male 42,054,459/ female 47,003,975)

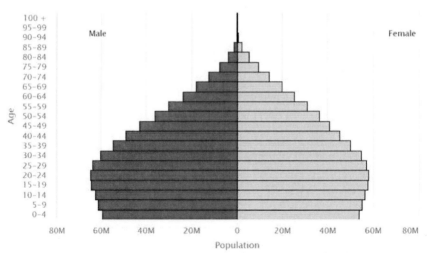

U.S. Census Bureau, International Database

General Comments on Education in India

True for much of Asia, as a generalization, education and the emphasis placed on ensuring that children diligently work on their education skills are highly embraced social norms for Indians. By observing a Chinese child's daily life we see that many 5- and 6-year-olds have a more stringent and rigorous work schedule than many western adults could tolerate. Indians come very close to this level of commitment with the grueling demand of a daily schedule populated by hours of study, class work, extracurricular tutoring, special private class work in math, sciences, and language, etc. It is a social norm in many India circles and of critical family importance. According to the World Economic Forum, PhD's earned by country breaks down as follows: according to an OECD report, the US has at least twice as many PhD graduates as Germany, its nearest rival. In 2014, 67,449 people graduated with a PhD in the US, compared to 28,147 in Germany. Next in line is the UK, which just pushes India into the third place with 25,020 PhD graduates. India had 24,300 PhD graduates.

Strain on the Infrastructure

Many of your team's resources emanate from the more rural parts of India moving into the urban hubs for better employment opportunities. This leads to congestion and higher living costs, as the demands grow in those areas for available housing and required services. As a result, there is an inevitable strain on the infrastructure including the roadways and transport systems, which carry your workers to their office locations. Average commute times in India show some very telling rising averages as both the population and impact on the roadways increase. The latest survey information gathered was from May 5, 2018. An average of 3 minutes per kilometer in this study. There are multiple articles over the years on this topic. I found the following table on an Indian Website: https://www.peoplematters.in/news/culture/indians-spend-7-of-their-day-in-office-commute-report-22905

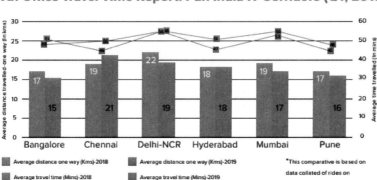

As the workers move further out from their office locations to find suitable housing at affordable prices, commuting becomes a significant factor in the availability of your work force. Thus, if an expert resource is required during off hours, it could take several hours for them to arrive at the office, as well as be informed of being required at the office. This reality must be factored into your user clients' and local staffs' mentality when things break. This is not unlike the same issue in the US outside of major urban commercial centers, but you must add to that understanding the following statement from Deepesh Agarwal, Co-Founder and CEO of New India Express:

India is constantly experiencing ongoing infrastructure development projects, which hamper the commute. There are plans being implemented to improve the traffic situation, but results are futile." He further added, "India is increasingly facing traffic woes, which have incidental impact to not just employees, but to employers and local authorities as well. (Agarwal 2021)

Although considering traffic congestion is unlikely to be up-front in an analysis of risk in your decision-making process, it is, in fact, a very real impact on the satisfaction and frustration levels that your staff and end users will experience as you make this transition. Enquiring with the potential team members about their daily commute – how they accomplish it, how long it takes them, and what their means in an emergency are – should be on your interview check list. I have had cases where the management leadership was in Chennai while their team was in Hyderabad. It took two months before I knew from one of the overwhelmed freshers that they never saw their manager. This was clearly the wrong time to gather that information. Further, it is not uncommon for your team member to not own a means of transport, such that they may share their commute with someone who may or may not be on your team at all. Thus, unplanned commutes are nearly impossible to overcome except by taxi or other very expensive and inconvenient means. Hence, these questions must be factored into your interviews as well.

As I go through my process in this book, I focus on three urban centers, namely Hyderabad, Bangalore, and Chennai. They are common outsource locations for many high tech and consultancies operating in the US and other Western nations and are the primary areas I experienced. I deduced that, regardless of the physical locations, they all share the same struggle with the common challenges of staffing. Moreover, you will encounter them, as my experience is not all that unique. Conflicts such as job hopping and resume shopping, creating high turnover, effective off hour supervision, leadership failures, and calendar conflicts will be a regular part of your work when managing the outsource team. Some of these issues can be solved with planning and good communication. Others are part of the very landscapes of these physical areas, as the working conditions tend to promote high turnover with many of the India's resource offices located on the same streets all connecting to the wild tangle of cables and telecom lines crisscrossing the streets like spider webs capturing bits of data that cascade through the jungle canopy of copper, fiber, and PVC.

Who is on your team?

Your support team will comprise a mix of "freshers", experts, product/application specialists, and leaders. I soon understood that I needed to know the mix of who was on my team and what level of skill they brought to the table. I developed a simple matrix to ensure that I knew who was on the team and what their level of competence was. It was not as obvious at first, but if you are contracting for 24 x 7 support, your weekends and off hours will not be as strong as your business operating hours. This means that you will get calls from your clients when things go sideways on Saturday nights and Sunday afternoons. It will be inevitable. The outsourcing company will populate your support team with those having the best language skills and highest expertise for those functional application(s) that happen to be overlapping your prime business hours and when the contacts at your company are most likely to be engaged with the support team for meetings, questions, problems, and functional support. The leadership will likely be available as escalation support by phone only by the support team. Thus, the freshers and less experienced team members will have to call the leadership/high level experts for help and hope that they can get them quickly when those experts are likely to be sleeping at home, out for the evening, or otherwise less available.

Some simple process things to do

- Develop a matrix by application of who supports your product and know who the senior level people are and who have less than 2 years of experience (Fresher) and each level between. I used a scale of 1 – 5: 1 and 2 being the freshers and less experienced, respectively, and 5 being an expert. Do this for every team member in every shift and have their contact information tested and working.

- If the application is complex and composed of multiple modules, ensure that you know how versed each team member is, not just by application, but by individual module within that application. A good example is Hyperion, a common financial planning and budgeting tool. This application has many components, and not every team member will be well-versed in each of the components of that application. Rank each member by their expertise by component. This will give you and your end user the right number/email to ping when something goes wrong or otherwise needs attention. Furthermore, it will highlight the weaknesses in your team that you may want to address.

- Your team will have high turnover, so ensure that you have a great recruiter who always support your support team with a good supply of personnel in the queue. It is in the nature of the support in India that team members will leave.

- When you interview, use video online techniques. Ironically, some of the less scrupulous have professional interviewers handling the introductory/hiring process and later substituting others for the actual team assignment.

- Simply raising the hourly pay does not stop job hopping. The new rate will be shopped in place of the old rate, and if the skill is in demand, the team member will be gone. If you really want to hold onto a particular team member, have a very detailed discussion with them so that you understand why they are leaving before simply tossing a new number out. Exit interviews are critical, and detailed information about the reasons must be carefully analyzed and incorporated into your next hiring decision.

SAMPLE PRODUCT SKILLS MATRIX											
Budgeting Office Financials											
First Shift Team (Client Work Hours)						Skill Level					Key Contact
TEAM MEMBER	YEARS Direct Support EXPERIENCE	CSS BASE	Period Close Mgt	SECURITY	DATA QUALITY	Client Language	Planning	Budgeting	Current Skills Up Grade		
R.A.	3	4	3	5	2	3	2	1	Course Work - Hyperion Budgeting	
R.B. Shift Supervisor	8	5	3	4	3	5	3	5	Course Work - Organizational Mgt	•
R.C. Alternate Supervisor	5	2	2	3	5	5	2	3	Course Work - Planning	
R.D.	2	2	1	3	1	5	2	2	Course Work - Security Server Level	
R.L.	1	1	1	1	1	2	2	3	Language Classes	
R.M.	1	2	3	5	4	2	3	4	Language Classes	
R.S.	2	3	5	4	3	1	2	2		
R.P.	4	2	2	4	4	4	3	2	Course Work - Citrix & DBA Certification	
R.G.	4	5	3	3	5	3	2	2	Course Work - Hyperion Budgeting	
Skill Key: 1 Fresher 2 Low 3 Intermediate 4 High 5 Expert											

The skills matrix can be as detailed or as simple as you feel appropriate, but it is critical that you have a good understanding of the team and the skills they possess across the menu of products and systems you have within their care. Take the time to build this knowledge and keep it up to date. It becomes a benchmark for rating their performance, and should you establish a pay for performance management tool, it becomes a way to rank their earnings against those metrics. Keep track of their performance through an integrated ticketing system.

A cautionary note here, as I have mentioned a ticketing system above. Of course, this is standard practice and very much a part of IT methodology. Be detail oriented when you build your performance expectations, as well as on your intention to rank and rate that performance using a ticketing system. Be careful not to fall into a trap of counting the number of tickets generated in a period, for instance, "N number of tickets are included as part of the service fee per month". Such a metric bogs down and becomes meaningless as time goes on. You must define the type of tickets. A ticket can be generated every time you add a new employee to get them loaded into and on boarded into the system with access security and access permissions. So what? This has nothing to do with the performance of the system: it is just the paperwork required to on board someone new or change the status of an existing employee to access into and out of some other system. It is better to measure the time taken to execute such tickets that we shall call "administrative actions". As opposed to counting the number of tickets, tracking the time taken to execute and complete such tickets tells us a great deal. Is our on boarding demand unreasonable? Is our on boarding process too cumbersome? Where are the "overweight tasks" in the process? Are they necessary? These are the more important metrics to gather from the performance review, and simply counting the tickets gives us nothing to improve. For this discussion, it is important to note that this will be a considerable area of diligence and assessment to delve into. For now, and our purposes in this book, know that this area will be a significant and on-going challenge that demands a great deal of up-front thought and detail before signing the deal.

On-Site/Local Support from your Outsource Team

Part of your outsourcing will likely require some amount of on-site support at least during some special conditions or projects that can arise at your company. These can include resources that require work visas, and there have been times when obtaining these visas were not routine in anyway. Political implications could impact the timing and availability of such visas. Thus, it is wise to establish a local recruiter who specializes in temporary local resources, and build that into the outsource contract, such that you can integrate such resources into the outsource team if there are any security or special access rules needed to be followed. Moreover, having a local with Indian language skills is a good idea if you have the luxury of finding such temporary workers. Have rates negotiated as best you can proactively, as these resources can be very expensive on an emergency basis, and you may not have the ability to avoid those situations. Furthermore, one should consider having a contract with temporary housing companies that can locate and lease apartments for the on-site location resources because housing on-site resources at hotels is expensive, and if longer than a few weeks at a time, very disheartening to the temporary worker who is trapped in a hotel room for weeks on end. It will also save you a lot of money, as you are not paying the hotel room and restaurant rates for food and laundry.

Bear in mind that many of these resources who locate for a first time to a temporary project view the dollars and compare it to their home country's economic realities. They believe to have hit jackpot and be able to help family and friends with the wealth of a western pay rate. What they do not realize is that the cost of living will absorb most if not all of that "windfall" and force them in a small hotel/motel probably shared with one or two other resources and no automobile. Be sensitive to this, as reality will hit them very hard a week or so after they arrive on site. This combined with being homesick and a bit overwhelmed by the newness of the place, food, and living style can demoralize and possibly have some resources looking to return home soon after their arrival.

Chapter 3

The Economy of India

Much like the case with most other countries, India's economy also took the expected hits due to the outbreak of COVID and the world's reaction to it through shutdowns and restrictions on travel and trade. Prior to COVID, India's economy was enjoying a substantial annual increase above 7%. This growth has mostly continued although India has 25% of its population living in poverty. This dichotomy is extensive and pervasive. There is an underlying social tension that this separation creates, but to India's credit, outbreaks of civil unrest have not occurred in any but a few of the most contentious states, such as Nagaland, K & J, and certain excursion areas along its borders. More of this discussion is covered in later chapters where we examine the risks of terrorism and related militaristic issues impacting India. There have been upheavals in the agricultural sector of the economy that culminated in a farmers' march that sought better government protections and subsidies as part of India's overall economic policy. The march ended peacefully, and some concessions were made quelling further disruptions in that sector of the economy.

India's economy is relatively stable, considering the challenges it faces. A review of economic analysis by the World Bank and Indian internal Ministry of Finance reflects this stability. I have added a few links that can point you to the specific reports for your review. This does not mean that the Indian economy does not face some large challenges. The World Economic Forum has an excellent article (https://www.weforum.org/agenda/2019/01/India-biggest-future-three-challenges-consumption/) covering these challenges in some detail. It is wise to be aware of these challenges.

Simply stated, the challenges are as follows: Skills Development and "Re-Skilling" current workers to better fit into the future economic needs of the nation and the world; the improvement of, thus far, marginally successful efforts to teach and raise skill levels of the rural poor areas of India; and meeting a sustainable growth, which will both support the population's demands and needs for health and reasonable livable conditions within its exploding urban centers. Chennai has seen a significant impact in this area. The rapid and often "unsupervised" growth and build out of this city has created a devastating impact on its ground water and increased the lower city flood plains. As a result, the ocean is infiltrating the ground water and causing a major environmental and living condition problem. Be mindful of this location and this situation, as efforts by the Indian government and local authorities have been unsuccessful at addressing this problem. Chennai is one of those urban areas that has had explosive growth well beyond the ability of its infrastructure, government, or environment. It has been unable to adapt to the changes imposed on the swamp water recharge area that later had often-corrupt building permits being handed out. These were handed out by authorities that were too eager to get their piece of the pie, circumventing ordinances and building codes for the "right" considerations.

India is awash in multinational programs aimed at improving various aspects of life from healthcare to education to infrastructure, environmental problems, and agriculture. A current list of active or recently attempted initiatives is listed at the end of this book. One of the significant issues has been attempts to close the large gap between the rural poor and growing urban skilled and educated populations. Initially, getting rural students into a classroom was itself a significant problem. When this became successful and students began attending school and occupying seats, the effort shifted to effectively teaching basic literacy and numeracy. A report issued in January of 2017 pointed out the failure of education programs in the rural poor populations. The following abstract is taken from a published report written by Abhishek Choudhary (https://thewire.in/education/india-primary-education-pratham-aser):

On the morning of July 15 2016, Uttar Pradesh chief minister, Akhilesh Yadav, found himself inside a primary school classroom in the northern district of Shravasti. Since the second half of 2016, all major parties in the northern state have been sharpening their strategy for the assembly election, which is due next month. Yadav had gone to Shravasti to launch Hausla Poshan Yojana, a new scheme aimed at improving nutrition among pregnant women and malnourished children, and to discuss the development supposedly achieved during his tenure.

The 'surprise visit' to the school came about mainly because it was within the compound where the scheme was to be launched. Once he was in the classroom, Yadav was shocked to learn that only one girl in the class could read a chapter from her Hindi textbook. The rest could not read a word, a report stated. (None of the reports on Yadav's Shravasti visit mentioned which grade these children belonged to, but since they were expected to read from a Hindi textbook, one could guess they were from the second or third grade.)

This incident captures much of what is wrong with India's popular approach to primary education. The school Yadav visited was equipped with basic infrastructure; it had a concrete building, the students all wore uniforms and had books. Yadav blamed the teachers for the children's inability to read from their textbooks, going so far as to say they were determined to ruin the entire upcoming generation.

A Non-Government Organization (NGO), Pratham (https://www.pratham.org/about/), stepped in. It is a highly successful NGO working in India, specifically within its education arena, that tested several innovation iterations after this incident. Some innovations developed and employed in this area have proven to be effective, but the challenges of local and national corruption have threatened to undermine those successes. A recent BBC article points directly to widespread corruption as part of the failings of why such programs do not work in India (https://www.bbc.com/news/world-south-asia-13447867). The long-term goal of continued growth and need to reduce the percentage in poverty seriously obstruct India's goals.

The World Bank says the public distribution program, which soaks up almost half the money, has brought limited benefits. It gives subsidized food and other goods to the poor. The report says one landmark scheme, launched more than five years ago, aims to guarantee government work for the rural unemployed. But the World Bank found that it was failing to have an impact in the poorest states because of under-payments and bad administration. All this is embarrassing for the Congress party, which leads the coalition government. It promised to reduce the gap between the small percentage of wealthy Indians and very large percentage of poor ones, who feel excluded from the economic boom. This report suggests that however good intentions may be, the delivery still needs a lot of work. Although India is seeing rapid growth, more than 40% of its population still lives below the poverty line. (J.McGivering, BBC News May 2011)

Culturally, India is foundationally tied to an embedded social structure of a large patchwork of local languages that is essentially a "village by village" religious system of doctrines and deities, and its resultant influence on local beliefs and decision-making. Hence, high levels of nepotism and highly regionalized political diversity isolates many states from the federal institutions. This tends to be true of any large nation including the US if, for example, we compare Alabama to Northern California or Massachusetts. However, in the US, we share a common language, and, for the most part, a legal structure that underpins a strong sense of baseline laws and a communication infrastructure that ensures better access to available information to nearly everyone in the US. This is not possible in India. The isolation, for instance, of Mumbai to Noklak in the Nagaland state is not easily overcome like in the case of, let's say, Washington DC to Coos Bay Oregon. Although this issue may not directly impact the outsourcing center in Bangalore, it does impact the long-term stability of India and the governance of a nation that has such vast cultural differences.

India boasts of economic strength owing to these differences and the resulting diversification of its economic resources. The question in the end will be if the central government can keep all these disparate parts of its whole intact as a blended and smoothly operating system of often conflicting parts? Can these disparate segments all sum together for the sake of a single nation, or do they fly apart from the strain? Not an easy task, especially if the local authorities do not share the vision.

Watching this struggle and measuring it in terms of how this risk impacts your operation are difficult metrics to get a handle on, but it is something to keep on the radar at least for warning signs and potential disastrous effects, should the seams begin to tear.

Researching the details of India's economy, I was able to notice many sources of detailed information. Given the variety of sources and volume of reports and studies and articles, ranging from basic commentary to in-depth reporting, I was able to contrast and compare, and, thus, build confidence that this data is presentable to you, the reader. The question became what was the best summary information? One such source that I believe raised the right questions and topics of value and stopped this book from becoming a lesson in economics is a publication called Global Edge. The following are the economic issues identified and reported by Global Edge (https://globaledge.msu.edu/countries/india/risk/):

- High corporate debt and non-performing assets (NPA)
- Net importer of energy resources
- Lack of adequate infrastructure
- Weak public finances
- Bureaucratic red tape, inefficient justice
- Widespread poverty, inequality, and informality
- Military confrontation in Kashmir with China and Pakistan
- Non-participation in regional trade agreements (Regional Comprehensive Economic Partnership Agreement)

If we break down the areas identified by Global Edge report, we can further understand the risks and what to watch for in the future. Let's take these areas separately, starting with NPA's, a significant issue in India impacting its economy.

• High corporate debt and non-performing assets (NPA)

The matter was deemed serious enough such that in 2022, India created and manned a department of uncollected debt reporting directly to the PM's office. Tracking this issue is relatively simple through a variety of resources. Making this part of your risk management strategy is critical and should not be overlooked, as the impact of NPA on the Indian economy can be severe and can produce long-term consequences. The following is an excerpt from a recent article in "Economic Times - India":

> *"The gross non-performing asset (GNPA) ratio of scheduled commercial banks is likely to increase to 9.5 per cent in September 2022 from 6.9 per cent in September 2021 in a severe stress scenario, the Reserve Bank of India (RBI) said on Wednesday."*

This places India high on the unenviable list of major economies with this critical underperforming segment of their banking system. Given that India just appointed a new administrator to address their bad loan directorate, I suspect some of this dirty laundry display is the strategy typical of a savvy manager bringing out all the worst news out before taking over the position. However, if the information is truly that dire, this does not portend well that solutions and achievements in addressing the issue are imminent. Do not expect miracles. There are near-term rocky roads to be expected here.

• Net importer of energy resources

A 2021 report on India's energy requirements (https://www.iea.org/reports/india-energy-outlook-2021) shows a serious inability to continue its growth rate and economic ability to absorb its requirement for energy. It will need to sustain its projected current path. An excerpt of this report is as follows:

India is the world's third-largest energy consuming country, thanks to rising incomes and improving standards of living. Energy use has doubled since 2000, with 80% of demand still being met by coal, oil, and solid biomass. On a per capita basis, India's energy use and emissions are less than half the world average, as are other key indicators such as vehicle ownership, steel, and cement output. As India recovers from a Covid-induced slump in 2020, it is re-entering a very dynamic period in its energy development. Over the coming years, millions of Indian households are set to buy new appliances, air conditioning units, and vehicles. India will soon become the world's most populous country, adding the equivalent of a city the size of Los Angeles to its urban population each year. To meet growth in electricity demand over the next twenty years, India will need to add a power system the size of the European Union to what it has now.

The recent 2022 news reports have placed India's reliance on Russian oil imports front and center for many of us despite the topic never having been on our radar in the past for anyone other than Intelligence and State Department experts who would track such details. However, it is on our list of items here to remind us to be aware and to add to our risk calculations. The real risk, beyond where the energy fuel source emanates from, is that India requires a massive amount of energy. That energy demand is growing year by year well beyond its capability to convert the fuel into to a useful and deliverable form for its residents and industries. The real metric lies in paying attention to India's infrastructure projects and its ability to deliver that energy where it is needed.

The Brookings Institute has published data on this specific risk segment that can be used for developing a metric. Their report, India's power distribution sector: An Assessment of Financial and Operational Sustainability was last published in October

2019 (https://www.brookings.edu/research/indias-power-sector-distribution). This particular study has been taken over in 2022 by Centre for Social and Economic Progress (CSEP) (https://csep.org/working-paper/a-hybrid-energy-input-output-table-for-india/#). Its level of detail and coverage in many aspects of policy concerning India, including its climate impacts and citizen access, among others, are extensive. This is a highly recommended source for anyone who wishes to deeply delve into the economics and public policy of India in terms of its energy policy. The bottom line for this risk is that India has a deep gap in its ability to provide for the energy needs of its nation in terms of infrastructure, specifically distribution. The real challenge is in how India invests and develops its ability to deliver power to its citizens' households and industries.

- Lack of adequate infrastructure

A simple search that asks the question of "what the infrastructure shortfalls in India are" produces dozens of responses. There is a good deal of political noise in these various reports supporting one party or viewpoint or another. Rather than attempting to sort out the motives of the speaker I have opted to separate out the political inferences injected into the topic about infrastructure project, investments, or priorities. I have been diligent to eliminate any statement that seemed rooted in rhetoric; this is not a simple task. To summarize, I am citing as neutrally as possible that I have eliminated any statements that would mention a particular political party positively or negatively. I want the water to be as clear as possible without any sediment stirred into it.

I created a rough spreadsheet to compare reports on infrastructure and where its goals versus actual achievements stand between 2012 and 2022. These data points are not numerically rich, but are, instead laced with narratives and observations. However, setting these various timeline narratives side by side, clearly signifies how the progress was slow, such that from 2016 to 2021, not much progress toward India's challenges in this area had been achieved. In 2021, this began to change with far greater levels of national and international investment in various projects, ranging from rail and dams to electrical grid and roadways. A resource I have located, Mordor Intelligence (https://www.mordorintelligence.com/about), is proving to be highly valuable in this area.

The following are some of the several key data points I have gleaned from their report on infrastructure:

- The Indian infrastructure is estimated to grow at a Compound Annual Growth Rate (CAGR) of approximately 7% during the forecast period.

- The Indian Government plans to invest about INR 102 lakh crores on infrastructure projects by 2024-25. The five-year-long National Infrastructure Pipeline (NIP) will enter its second year in FY 2021, during which INR 1,950,397 crores are to be invested. About INR 19.5 lakh crores have been budgeted during FY 2021 as part of the NIP. Urban infrastructure, road transport, energy, and Railways account for about 70% of allocation this 2020.

- About 42% of the projects in the NIP are under implementation, which means construction work is already undergoing. Another 19% is under a development stage, while 31% is still in its conceptual stage.

- Between the fiscal years 2020 and 2025, sectors such as Energy (24%), Roads (19%), Urban (16%), and Railways (13%) amount to around 70% of the projected capital expenditure in infrastructure in India.

For a deep dive into each of these infrastructure segments you can, connect with Mordor (https://www.mordorintelligence.com/industry-reports/infrastructure-sector-in-india#)

Infrastructure will be a problematic area for India for some years to come, ranging from housing within its urban centers to sanitation systems, energy grid distribution, water, transport systems, roadways, rail, etc. The continued population growth of India is expected to exceed that of China's in the next decade. The feeding, housing, and provision of services for India's citizens is guaranteed to significantly burden the nation's ability to deliver services and provide adequate financial and wage growth for majority of its citizens. Adding the expected pressure of meeting the environmental protocols, along with all these systemic issues, will certainly stretch the nation's ability to manage and absorb these demands.

- Weak public finances

To research the data around India's public debt, I relied and heavily weighed on three agencies, namely Fitch, Moody's, and S&P. S&P and Fitch provided a rating of BBB, while Moody's gave a slight uptick based on what they believe is a strengthening of control over India's expenditures. Fitch confirmed the baseline numbers for India's economic outlook for 2022 through 2026. All three agreed that a revision of their economic growth forecast was in order, and they revised their projections from a high 10+ percentage down to 9.5 percentage. Having factored the hit imposed worldwide due to Covid, India was further impacted by the substandard performance in the roll out of vaccinations. India's early stumbles with its vaccination program led to a longer recovery time for durable goods and consumer spending in India is hampered by low wages unlike other economies, such as, for instance, Korea's, where consumer purchases helped bridge a portion of the loss in revenue. It will be interesting to observe how the projections change due to inflationary pressures, especially in the energy sector. This is a metric well worth watching.

- Bureaucratic red tape, inefficient justice

Reuters published an article, dated to October 2018, showing how India had made major strides to improve its ability to work with businesses and ease the red tape involved in opening and operating a business in India (https://www.reuters.com/article/us-india-business-worldbank-idUSKCN1N525G). An excerpt showing the improvements that still stand is as follows:

NEW DELHI (Reuters) - Long known for its bureaucracy, India has made major strides in improving prospects for businesses in the country, the World Bank said in a report on Wednesday. India rose 23 places to 77th in the World Bank's Ease of Doing Business Index for 2019, up from 100th in 2018 and 130th in 2017, when it was ranked lower than Iran and Uganda.

The good news from the World Bank's report on improvements for India's business "friendliness" is only a part of this metric. Another, less directly impactful part of this metric concerns the legal system and how it disposes off court cases. This is unlikely to be of significant impact for our purposes here unless a rare condition comes up where you need to take legal action on behalf of someone or something in India. Understand that there are major inefficiencies and a great amount of challenge when it comes to litigious actions within India's court system. Should such a condition come up for you, it is highly advisable that your legal team make the appropriate contacts with local country experts. A valuable resource for back ground on this topic can be found within the Tata Foundation (www.tatatrusts.org/insights/survey-reports/**india-justice**-report).

- Widespread poverty, inequality, and informality

Again, although not a direct impact on this outsourcing discussion, it is wise to understand the potential disruptions due to social economic pressures. This can be an important factor for managing the relationship between your key leaders your employees. Instilling a certain empathy and consideration for the vastly different social conditions and circumstances that some of your team members will be shaped by will help temper and guide the interactions, especially those that are based on difficult or contentious moments every partnership is sure to encounter.

- Military confrontation in Kashmir with China and Pakistan

I have written a complete chapter on this topic, as it has a significant potential as a major disruptor to your outsourcing work.

- Non-participation in regional trade agreements (Regional Comprehensive Economic Partnership Agreement)

The Regional Comprehensive Economic Partnership (RCEP / ˈɑːrsɛp/ *AR-sep*) is a free trade agreement among the Asia-Pacific nations of Australia, Brunei, Cambodia, China, Indonesia, Japan, South Korea, Laos, Malaysia, Myanmar, New Zealand, the Philippines, Singapore, Thailand, and Vietnam.[2] The 15 member countries account for about 30% of both the world's population (2.2 billion people) as well as the global GDP ($29.7 trillion), thus making it the largest trade bloc in history. Signed in November 2020, RCEP is the first free trade agreement among the largest economies in Asia.

Subrahmanyam Jaishankar, India's Minister for External Affairs, recently argued that *"trade deals have led to deindustrialization"*. Further, he argued that in the face of India's drive to a "Made in India" policy, India could not accede to the agreement. Many have stated that this is a long-term folly on India's part: one that will isolate and prevent them from having a voice or stake in the agreement's maturation process. On the other hand, India argues that previous trade agreements have driven up their trade deficits with no clear benefit to India. Like other economic issues in India, this one requires close observation as it goes forward.

The recent historic inflation rates in India have largely been well controlled with a few notable spikes. This is a good data point to observe to avoid cost increase surprises.

Current and Historic Inflation Rates

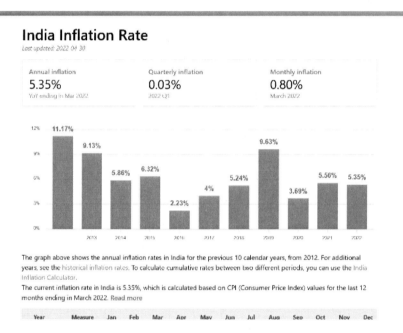

Chapter 4

Geological Risks

It was not possible to write about the risks of outsourcing in India without studying the geologic instability of this region. Due to following reasons, I find it hard to summarize the details of this risk: the science of geology, although I find it fascinating and as a child, I saw a possible future career in it for myself, is very foreign to me; and since the language and data expressed within the geologic writings that I have used for this study are voluminous, presenting a complete summary is far outside from the scope of this work. Consequently, I have restricted my writing to some of the basic data behind the geologic structure of the region and its likely higher risk locations due to this underlying seismic structure. The most basic description is a given that most people have some knowledge of it, i.e., India is an underlying tectonic plate that is moving northward at about 1 foot per year and colliding with the Asian continent, thus creating enormous folds in the land mass: the Himalayan Mountains are the most visible indication of the forces at work here. This movement has and continues to cause a great deal of instability on both sides of that collision. India is a subduction zone sliding under the Asian plate. This activity has been documented over decades of study beginning in the late 19th century with revisions to those findings as the science and tools of geologic structure continues to be upgraded and refined. A rich source of data is available in Ram S. Sharma's work as presented in his book *"Cratons and Fold Belts of India."* India, in short, is a highly active seismic area of the world. Understanding the geologic conditions of India is essential to any decision process involving the placement of critical systems and knowledge cache within this area. Failing to do so jeopardizes the long-term viability of such systems and resources.

https://www.mapsofindia.com/maps/india/seismiczone.htm provides a good resource for reviewing these resources. I have adapted some of this data to include an overlay of the typical urban areas where many of the outsourcing resources and activities occur. The good news is that the three key cities cited in this writing all lie within Zone I or II seismic areas where the risk of earthquakes is the lowest. Although this does not make them immune to such events, it lessens the likelihood. The issues that remain are, primarily, the other disasters that can affect these key locations and, secondarily, the nation's ability or lack thereof to handle large scale events in those areas where earthquake activity is a higher zone risk. There are many such areas with substantial populations. As mentioned earlier, the first responders are often not equipped to handle such events, thereby transferring the resources of less impacted areas to respond to the higher impacted areas. This is not unlike many nations one can argue, as for example, large scale fires in the western US require the resources of many other areas of the nation to lend assistance by way of equipment and human capital. The difference is that India does not have the infrastructure to make such lending arrangements in a timely or coordinated manner due to lack of communication systems, trained personnel, and/or equipment. Therefore, any serious natural event impacts all areas of the nation in a very direct manner.

According to India's National Institute of Disaster Management,

Almost 85 percent of the country is vulnerable to one or more hazards such as earthquakes, floods, droughts, cyclones, and landslides. More than 50 million people are affected by natural disasters annually.

Interestingly, one of the critical outsourcing areas, Hyderabad, an area with a low likelihood of earthquake disaster threat, ranks among the highest areas of natural disaster:

The few states with functioning state disaster management authorities, such as Odisha, Andhra Pradesh, Gujara,t and Bihar, are the ones with the most serious history of natural disasters, said Dhar Chakraborti[11].

A recent article in the Economic Times (Aug 7, 2021) stated the following:

While India was more or less prepared for the multiple heat waves and five cyclones that made landfall during the pandemic, mainly due to better forecasting, the country is still short of a robust mechanism to respond in advance to natural disasters such as landslides, flash floods, and even lightning strikes.

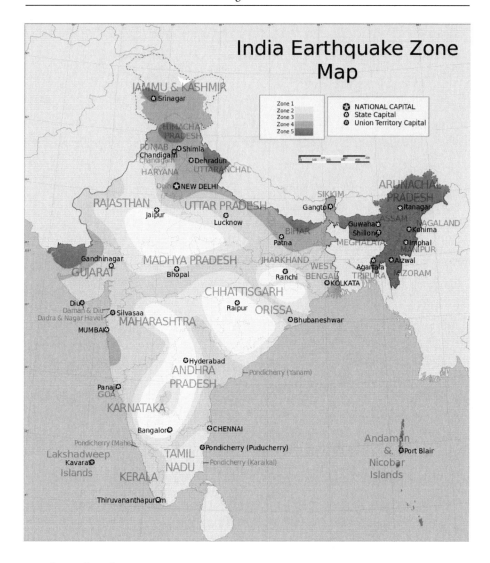

Hyderabad

The National Disaster Management organization has linked Hyderabad to a monitoring system functioning 24 x 7. The expectation is that responses to a disaster would be timely and sufficient for the event. Let us review the actual results of such responses. Reviewing a list of recent incidents in Hyderabad from newspaper sources along with commentary brings to light the following:

Hyderabad has a history of severe floods with substantial property damage and loss of life primarily due to the formation of cyclones in the Bay of Bengal and the resultant heavy rainfall that then overwhelms and overflows the banks of the Musi. A series of flood control gates and measures are in place on the river but a part of the lowland sectors of the city suffers regular evacuation mandates due to flooding threats. 2020 and 2021 were very active years for flooding events. This is mainly due to rainfall driven by the Bay of Bengal and the resultant need to open the flood control systems on the river, which impacts the downstream housing areas of the city. In October of 2020, floods claimed 50 lives in Hyderabad. The flooding incident of August 1, 2021 was the latest that succeeded the October 2020 event. It caused the government to ask people to remain home for a 2-day unplanned holiday due to the flooding. Previous events dating back to the early 20th century have seen significant loss of property and life in Hyderabad. At one point in the early 1900s, nearly a quarter of the population of the city was rendered homeless in one such flooding event. The following detail has been assembled in the https://orangenews9. com/annual-floods-natural-disasters-or-manmade/:

For example, every year since 2015, "Floods" and the havoc caused in Hyderabad have made headlines to include: September 29/30, 2016, 16.7 cm rain breaks 16-year-old record; and flood many colonies; Oct 8,2017 – Heavy rains flood many colonies and Telengana, third most vulnerable to flooding; Aug 21, 2018 — flooding of many low lying colonies; 2019 – record rain and heavy flooding brought life to a crippling halt, killing at least 15 people and causing water logging in various parts of the city, and now the latest flooding in 2020.

In 1950s and even up to 1970s, Hyderabad was known as the "City of Lakes" – nearly 3000 lakes. More than 50 per cent of them have disappeared. In one decade, Hyderabad lost about 3245 acres of water bodies. It is estimated that there were 932 tanks in 1973 in and around Hyderabad, which came down to 834 in 1996. Consequently, the area under water bodies got reduced from 118 to 110 sq.km. About 18 water bodies of over 10-hectare size and 80 tanks of below 10-hectare size were lost during that period. A yet another study on land use/land cover for Hyderabad and a large area around reveals that the area under water bodies has come down from 2.51 per cent of the geographical area in 1964 to 2.40 per cent in 1974 and to 1.57 per cent in 1990. The decline during 1974-90 periods has been sharp; now it is sharper with rapid growth due to massive development since 1990 with water bodies declining over time due to urban sprawl.

In their place, "Mega Building Structures" have been sanctioned by the GHMC to come up. For example, today, adjoining the highway to Patancheruvu near Chandanagar, the two lakes – Gangaram Cheruvu and Bhachuu Kunta Cheruvu – stand as a testimony to the havoc of creation of "Cement Jungles". Even the Alwal Lakebed encroachments are living examples with the outflow canals to Tirumulgherry inhabited by authorized colonies since 1970s up to Bon Cheruvu in Tirumulgherry area and beyond.

There were 169 large water bodies to include: Husain Sagar, Osman Sagar, Himayat Sagar, Shamirpet Lake, Mir Alam Tank, Safilguda Lake, Ramakrishnapuram Lake, Kapra Lake, and so on. HUDA, in first phase, proposed to restore 87 lakes. But what are the realities? The 2019 Hyderabad Bachao Twitter report "Rocks Bachao, Lakes Bachao, Heritage Bachao, and Errum Manzil Bachao. This is a shout out to all those who have been fretting about how Hyderabad has been changing rapidly." Surely, the State Government is culpable of turning a "Blind Eye" to civil society warnings repeatedly. And, then blame nature for the woes on annual basis.

In Hyderabad, the root causes for colonies submerged by floods on annual basis is simple. It is the collusion of the local political leadership directing GHMC officials to sanction buildings in low lying areas violating "Master Plans" resulting in near total concretization of city, unauthorized encroachment into lake beds, sanctioning buildings in low lying areas and their outflow canals, abject failure in provisioning adequate rainwater drainage pipelines (sizes), non-implementation of scientific water harvesting structures, etc."

Flooding disasters are very likely to grow in Hyderabad, considering the ever-increasing impact on property and people based on these past experiences, the short-sighted building policies, and the easily corrupted abuse of the controlling authorities within the government framework in this area. This is a risk area that needs to be part of the decision-making process although it is based on a more esoteric measurement in terms of natural disaster potentials. The potential for infrastructure and human capital loss is significant with either of those conditions having a direct impact on one's ability to operate effectively and without disruption.

Bangalore

Like Hyderabad, Bangalore is a significant location for outsourced workers and infrastructure. It too shares a link in the Rural Disaster Management System of India where it is subject to high danger of floods and loss of property and life. Moreover, like Hyderabad, it is in a Zone I/II area where earthquake is at the low end of the seismic threat scale. Although this is good news, once again, it does not guarantee an immunity from such seismic activity.

Bangalore suffers from the same local challenges as Hyderabad in skirting good practices in terms of land use and building codes. The push to increase capacity and capture more of the international funds flowing into the nation from around the globe, especially from western tech organizations, places a very high level of pressure on local economic drivers who are hungry for those currencies and employment opportunities. The questions then are what are the costs in terms of risk and how often can one expect to suffer a calamity? According to research, this risk can be significant. Flooding tops the list of disasters to this region. The August 2019 statistics include the following details:

Damages due to flooding in Karnataka: data released by Karnataka Chief Minister's Office

- Human lives lost: 61

- People Missing: 15

- Animal death: 859

- People evacuated: 697,948

- Animals rescued :51,460

- Relief camps opened: 1,160

- People in relief camps: 396,617

- Houses damaged: 56,381

- Districts and Taluks* (*Indian revenue district) affected: 103 taluks of 22 districts affected

- Loss of Agriculture and Horticulture crop (preliminary assessment): 6.9 lakh hectares.

A key component of disaster management involves the ability to locate the affected areas quickly and accurately. In the western nations GIS and the implementation of DigitalOcean has been a widespread tool to establish a grid system for implementing such management tools. In India, this implementation has been stalled due to lack of action in many key areas. A recent statement by a leading practitioner of DigitalOcean, Praveen Bhaniramka, co-founder of the Gurgaon-based startup stated the following concerning Bangalore:

> Geospatial information is a key element in disaster management...It is high time for the city administration to use GIS-based data to reach decisions. If civic agencies identify issues and put that data in the public domain, it will benefit every citizen.[12]

He continued that the BBMP had no way to publish such data at present.

> "I found that efforts to deploy GIS have been seriously attempted and documented in some areas and key urban locations throughout India. Some of these efforts are well documented with solid project goals and public information sources. Others have not been as thorough in their implementation efforts".

An example of a well-defined and thought-out deployment concerns New Delhi. The public portal with white paper and documentation is linked here: https://www.int-arch-photogramm-remote-sens-spatial-inf-sci.net/XLII-2-W7/49/2017/isprs-archives-XLII-2-W7-49-2017.pdf

Chennai

Again, much like Hyderabad, Chennai suffers from flooding as a primary driver of disasters primarily due to urban development without attention to planning and impact on the placement of such construction. It is a rush to capture as many international funds as possible beyond the planning and policy of good governance.

Chennai is situated on a coastal area where urban development can only expand in a north or south orientation. The city was originally a seacoast fishing village with a few settlements. The increase of this city has exceeded 20% of its original size in a few short years. It could not possibly be expected to absorb such a massive change in its infrastructure without creating problems well beyond the local government's ability to control or plan properly for such expansion. The results are not surprising then that the freshwater table has been intruded by salt water, and the "flood sink" in the southern portion of the city has been virtually overwhelmed by the massive increase in water shed on paved surfaces that now act as riverways draining a city that went from 5.3 million people in 2001 to 9 million people in less than 10 years and now over 11 million in 2019. There is a civic population lead effort to "save the wetland," but with little substantial government involvement, it is not likely to produce any significant results beyond the political impact on local elections. For a detailed discussion with tables and data concerning the changes to land use, refer the article by Sushmita Sengupta dated 12/3/2015 (https://www.downtoearth.org.in/news/natural-disasters/why-chennai-floods-are-a-man-made-disaster-51980).

As mentioned, the 2019 population of Chennai has grown to about 11 million. The loss of the water table and subsequent drought conditions it has produced, along with a loss of water for the local population, promises to gate any future expansion or even the city's ability to sustain its current population. Of the three key cities we have talked about in this volume, it is highly likely that this city and its current crisis is the most threatening and near-term impacted area. People cannot live without a good water source. Unfortunately, this is purely a manmade crisis excluding even the ongoing typical Indian disasters of flooding, earthquake, tsunami, and cyclones. Let us not forget that Chennai is a coastal city and a Zone II earthquake seismic zone, placing it at a higher risk for any of these disasters than Hyderabad or Bangalore. My interjection here, without tipping my hand concerning how I see the global climate issues, is that we created and cannot get our arms around the water crisis of a single Indian city, but we're somehow planning to resolve the global climate issue.

In 2004, Chennai suffered a massive loss of life due to the Tsunami that devastated Indonesia and large areas of Tamil Nadu in India with over 8,000 lives lost. This risk remains, and, perhaps, beyond better warning systems of impending surges, there is no defense to be offered in such an event.

The summary of these cities and the risk they represent is that India is being overwhelmed by its own success in bringing international funds primarily for the benefit of western technology companies seeking cheap labor dollars. The impact includes population expansion at unsustainable levels and beyond the resource capabilities of the local governments in terms of infrastructure, civilian safety, and maintenance of good governance. This happens by overstepping or outright ignoring local ordinances, building codes, and impacting basic resources, such as fresh water supplies. These are highly short-sighted and greed-driven outcomes from a local government more interested in feathering their own nests than providing long-term benefits to the local citizenry. The major concerns for the users of such a system are the long-term stability and continuation of the companies and stake holders of those they are working to support and benefit. This is a chain link far overstretched and considerably weakened by overuse and limitation of its physical capabilities.

Chapter 5

Technological Benefits

One of the benefits we seek when outsourcing includes tapping the brain power and experience of the outsource provider. The idea is that as a company, we outsource once if everything goes well. However, the outsource provider does this multiple times and brings their experience and knowledge to the table. We get to benefit from the success of others without suffering the experience of the failures they likely went through and the cost of iterations. This is of course a primary attractor to this process and a guide as to why we select one provider over another. Perhaps they share our industry and the regulatory and statutory demands we must comply with. If we select the right provider, we immediately make those gains and minimize the learning curves and inherent risks of being a first-time practitioner.

Behind these obvious benefits is a desire to capitalize the provider's brain power and vision. We know that there is always a horizon. It is the nature of technology that the next best thing is always around the corner. We may not want to be the tip of the spear with the costs, guesses, and risks of that position, but we also do not want to be the last to the party. This questions the adeptness of our provider, and how in-tune they are with the next leap in technology? Are they poised and capable of bringing your game up by a level or two?

For this question, I made some assumptions including the application of machine learning, artificial intelligence, and self-diagnosing systems and where India ranks in comparison to other nations in these areas. How deep is their experience and ability to enhance your deployment when it comes to these near horizon abilities? Upon researching these current questions, I was surprised that India is nowhere near the front runners. The leader boards may or may not surprise you depending upon how closely you have been monitoring these developments. The question you will have to answer is one of competitive edge and cost benefit. The tradeoff will be how close your field of competitors are to migrating to systems that utilize these technological advances versus the cost of migrating to them and is your outsourcer capable of bringing you up to that level. My point in bringing this topic into a book concerning risk is to question how important it is for and you and your company to take advantage of these technologies?

In a recent article published by "Tortoise", (https://www.tortoisemedia.com/) a UK based collaborative news organization founded by a former BBC news director and a Times editor as an alternate news media outlet, I found an interesting "index" formula being used to track global leaders in these technologies. The Tortoise Index picks China as the rising star. Although the US still maintains its lead in this area according to indices employed by Tortoise, China is predicted to surpass them within the next 10 years. Meanwhile, China has overtaken the UK to the 2nd spot according to the index published in 2020. China has access to a vast amount of raw data unavailable to many other nations owing to China's population with cell phones and other online devices, as well as the lack of regulatory and statutory limitations on their access to the personal data. Additionally, investment in this area are encouraged and endorsed by the highest level of government, thus resulting in many resources from educational institutions to corporate entities to private citizenry being poured into this technology. It is a tidal wave of effort and focus so far unmatched anywhere else in the world.

The "Global AI Index" link on Tortoise is here: (https://www.tortoisemedia.com/intelligence/global-ai/): the first index to benchmark nations on their level of investment, innovation, and implementation of artificial intelligence.

I have not copied in this index due to its complexity and the benefit of viewing and reading it online so you can make use of the various toggles and filters it offers. I highly recommend your use of this resource.

Adaptation of Current Technology and Future Position

Our effort to outsource can bring benefits beyond just the primary cost savings driver. One such possibility is the outsourcers' ability to add to the value of their services by improving on our technology. For example, Oracle can add self-administering database management capabilities. If properly implemented and maintained, the reduction in the need for multiple DBA's can be a significant savings in personnel costs, 24x7 coverage, and consistent practice. These are highly desirable operational advances well worth the investment. They are not, however, permanent solutions. Such code driven functionalities will be leapfrogged and replaced in the short term as AI/Machine learning capabilities come online. The question then becomes whether the operational organizations, contracted to serve our outsourcing needs implement, and manage such new technologies? More importantly, are these organizations supported by the infrastructure of training schools/universities leading to the next generation of these technologies? This then questions where India stands in this race to the next level? Are they producing the thought leadership and industrial base required to push these concepts forward? If not, are we strapping ourselves to a train that has already lost the race and is heading for a dead end?

Additionally, this entire area of the next technological leap expected as a result of machine learning and the increase in our ability to manufacture and deploy AI-based chipsets, sets us apart from other nations, considering our base of manufacturing and the gap we enjoy in the US' abilities and infrastructure in this area. Additional to this, we act to maintain this gap between ourselves and the primary competitor, China, in this arena through the restrictions that the US has placed on all forms and means of export of any technology deemed part of our national defense and security. The resultant escalation of this "technology war" between the US and China is well summarized and discussed in Ernst Dieter's white paper released in 2020 by the Center for International Governance Innovation. It is a highly recommended read for anyone who would begin to invest time and resources into AI, especially chipset manufacturing. The interesting facet of this technological "gap" is that China has the rudimentary ability to far outpace the rest of the AI-competing world. This is in terms of their ability to capture data and create a massive base to build algorithms from owing to their population advantage and political ability to gather data without any significant legal restriction from its citizens. On the other hand, they do not have a robust AI chipset manufacturing foundation, and their current advancement plan in this technology, endorsed at the highest level of government, is presently stymied because of this US-lead technology war.

Chapter 6

Geopolitical (in) Stability and Risks

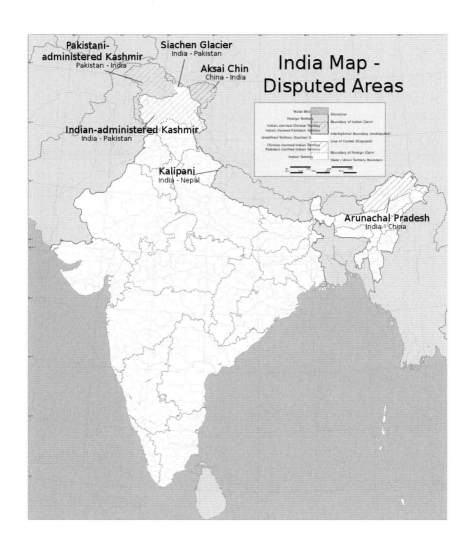

India faces several difficult challenges in this area. We typically think of two primary border areas that cause the most visible challenges: firstly, its partitioning partner, Pakistan, which shares a 3,323-kilometer (2,065 mi.) border; and secondly, China. The India-China border is less well-defined than the India-Pakistan border due to the historical fluctuations and claims by the British, which were never clearly addressed with China at the time. This ambiguity has led to some of the conflicts we see today in the Aksai Chin region. Further, the fluid control of these border regions are muddied due to both Britain and China's various military actions with the indigenous peoples in these areas. Wiki provides a good historical summary of these border issues, which are worth reading for highlights. Several volumes with extensive detail and scholarly research can be found there and in the detailed bibliography of this book

In 2014, a collection of essays and white papers were brought together concerning the future of India over the course of the next several decades up to a projected 2030. This seminal volume was written by several people within the Institute for Defense Studies & Analysis and compiled and edited by Brig Rumel Dahiya (retired) & Ashok K Behuria, PhD. It is a foundational resource for attaining a sense of the challenges and directions anticipated by this group within the context of the current technological and political world within which India must position itself to successfully navigate toward India's best interests.

I avoided making this topic a history lesson in the India-China border challenges and instead opted to list the various, and multiple, conflicts India deals with in the context of the risks of operating in India today. These are the conflicts you should be aware of and track to some degree as you go forward with your outsourcing efforts. The Pakistani and Chinese border issues, while the most significant military concerns, are not the only risk areas in terms of the geopolitical problems within India.

The security of India is far from a given. There are several very enlightening articles and essays written by Lt Gen Kamal Davar (retd) ranging from an assessment of external threats to internal conflicts and disputes that that disrupt India's long-term security. His essays are worth reading and can be found online with a quick search of his name. I encourage you to read the pertinent articles, especially those on Indian security. It could be difficult for western, especially North American nations, to understand this, given our tremendous luxury of being relatively isolated from hostile forces with any sizeable conventional military ability to inflict real harm within our hemisphere and such hostile states simply do not exist on our borders. Perhaps 9-11 is the best example to get a sense of what it would feel like to live under such continual and capable threats keeping in mind that the ability of anyone with hostile intentions to repeat such an attack is not impossible, but it is highly unlikely to reoccur with any frequency. For here in North America, we live in a typically stable and safe place on Earth.

This does not mean that we will not suffer calamities and severe attacks, 9/11 as the example of course and, perhaps our southern border brethren due to desperate population influxes without going into the politics of that situation. Besides, we have our own geological issues to deal with, but our ability to circumvent such impactful disruptions with highly trained and resource-rich teams far exceeds the abilities and capabilities of most other nations on Earth. Note that when such calamities strike, American teams are dispatched to anyplace on the planet to assist in the recovery operations. India survives in quite a different set of circumstances and realities. Threats from active terrorists on their borders in a multitude of disputed territories and incursions across their borders from outside nations is an on-going reality for India. Internally, India continues to feel the pressure of disputes requiring significant resources to maintain peace and repel repeated incursions and conflicts. Nagaland is a good example of these disputes and their impact on the nation. Despite a Modi-sponsored treaty between Nagaland and the central government of India signed in 2015, the conflict still rages on. A recent incident where an Assam government official and his escort were fired upon as recently as May 2021[8] by what is believed to be Naga forces who have pushed into the disputed area. This on-going Intra-India State border dispute has given rise to the potential use of drone surveillance to calculate the influx of Nagaland population into a forest reserve area. Imagine if such a dispute arose between, let's say, Massachusetts and Rhode Island.

As of this writing, the disputed areas in Northern India have had incursions and conflicts with China resulting in casualties and rising tensions promising more military activity. Groups that are funded and politically supported by Pakistan are active in several areas within Indian borders on a regular basis that cost human lives and opportunities for the growth and economic progress of its citizens. While the Western nations including North America are not immune from targeted terrorist actions, they tend to be isolated groups and for the most part, although tragic, do not disrupt our day-to-day operations. India, on the other hand, must continually be prepared for local actions preventing a peaceful and secure existence in multiple sectors of the nation.

Internal Threats

Readiness of First Responders and Military Forces

In 2019, India's police force was ranked among the weakest under a United Nations suggested level of 1 to 222. The inability of the states to adequately and successfully hire and train new recruits has left the nation with well above 30% shortfall in filling open slots for its police forces. Part of the issue lies in India's inability to reform its police due to the complicated organization and conflicting structure responsible for the police throughout the nation. I suggest reading this article, as it provides insights into the ongoing and systemic issues that create the dysfunction within the police forces across India (https://www.yourarticlelibrary. com/india-2/challenges-faced-by-police-organisations-in-india/46699).

In short, a bureaucratic control of the police by the Home Union ties the hands of both state and local police organizations from reforming their organizations due to overlapping responsibilities with no responsibility for the actual hiring and control of police. The result is that reforms have essentially remained undone since the Criminal Procedure Code of India, the Code of Civil Procedure, and the Indian Evidence Act dating back to 1861.

The inadequacies of these resources will be significantly compounded when confronted with calamity and threat to human life and property, let alone the numerous demands of any society dealing with a massive population including criminal behavior and the havoc and damage such behavior can wreak on the public at large. Simply put, the police cannot be counted on for relief in these moments.

Assessing the ability of the first responders when approaching this risk from a local/internal perspective before examining the external or national ability to respond to significant events is a good place to start. When talking about the stability of a nation, its internal systems, and ability to respond to critical threats and calamities, local law enforcement plays an important part in the nation's ability to promote and maintain peace, ensure a suitable environment for the population's safety, and promote the continuance of commerce without disruption. Here are some notable facts about the frailty of India's internal law enforcement infrastructure according to N.N. Vohra's work [1]:

- 25% of India's police stations and 50% of police outposts do not have regular buildings.

- Over 37% of police work from makeshift lines.

- Over 70% of police districts do not have proper control rooms.

- 34% of police superintendents do not have residential accommodations within the districts they oversee.

- 70% of the constabulary do not have accommodations.

- 43% of the mobility of the force is deficient.

- Weaponry is primarily obsolete or insufficient.

- Communication systems are out of date, inadequate, or not functioning.

- The National Police Commission has set standards for training but have achieved few if any of these standards.

  o Up-dated training every five years but achieved less than every 20 years if even then.

  o Workday of no more than 13 hours on shift but often exceed 20 hours.

  o Revised and up-dated guidelines for modern practices but are seldom reviewed or changed.

  o Forensic science labs are few and those that exist are seldom, if ever, updated.

These statistics are important to this study, as they indicate the underlying frailty of a system that can easily be overwhelmed in a significant event whatever be the root cause: geologic, criminal, internal corruption, disease, social up-risings, etc. This facet of risk does not include external military or terrorist incursions, as those would be handled by the Indian armed forces, and this specific risk factor only assesses internal police-related responses or rather, inability to effectively respond to such events.

An Executive Summary of Crime (Source: India National Crime Reporting Board – NCRB 2018)

i. *A total of 8,02,267 cognizable crimes comprising 545,502 Indian Penal Code (IPC) crimes and 256,765 Special & Local Laws (SLL[3]) crimes were registered in 19 metropolitan cities during 2018, showing an increase of 10.0% over 2017 (729,174 cases).*

ii. *During 2018, IPC[4] crimes have increased by 3.5% and SLL crimes have increased by 27.1% over 2017.*

iii. *Percentage share of IPC was 68.0%, while percentage share of SLL cases was 32.0% during 2018.*

iv. *Under IPC crimes, majority of cases were registered under theft accounting for 44.8% (244,159 out of 545,502 cases), followed by Rash Driving on Public way with 11.2% (61,177 cases), and hurt with 8.4% (45,584 cases) during 2018. Under SLL crimes, majority of cases were registered under Prohibition Act accounting for 25.3% (65,003 out of 256,765 cases), followed by City/Town Police Acts accounting for 23.4% (59,955 cases), and Motor Vehicle Act accounting for 7.6% 14(19,641 cases) during 2018.*

Movements and efforts to reform the police administration have been pursued since the late 1970's with little progress. The issue described as 'political interference' enables the assignment of less than qualified state leadership due to political loyalty or nepotism rather than careful placement to ensure capable and competent leadership in these important first responder positions. The results have driven the moral and confidence down within the ranks, as well as the population in general. The results have been negligible, and the published reports are *"collecting dust in the home ministry*"[5]. The complexities of these internal law enforcement issues run deep. The entanglement of political interests, criminal influence and control, and lack of attention by both the local governments and national infrastructure signal very few, if any, substantial improvements to come anytime soon.

Unfortunately, the military is called upon for many events, which should be handled by local police. This tendency facilitates the local governments to pass on their responsibilities to a central government rather than maintain local control and provide more immediate responses. In response, the central government began fielding multiple organizations with various assigned duties and overlapping authorities. The net result has been an inefficient use of funding, shifting already limited funds into smaller and smaller line items, and stifling any chance for an organization to update and improve its capabilities. Instead, these deficient organizations are forced to compete for a piece of a smaller pie under the political control of bureaucrats who possess narrow views within their own self interests. In the end, no one benefits, and the population of citizens and entities are ostensibly under the protection of a security force that is like the small-town fire departments in the west who are known to show up to "water down the foundations of the long since burned down buildings". The failure to protect significant infrastructure under the auspices of local government can cost millions in lost economic development and numerous lives because they simply do not have the resources or tools needed due to an over-division of duties and siphoning off of limited available resources.

External Threats

India's internal environment suffers from a range of significant tense conflicts within its borders by armed separatist groups and an internal security force that is ill-equipped to deal with such potentially explosive conditions. Additionally, it must also contend the external threats from the well-funded and capable military rivals along its borders. India shares borders with nations that have well-developed military capabilities and hostile intent, or, at a minimum, substantial interest in seeing India fail as an economy. Pakistan and China are among the primary nations holding grudges with India, while other nations in these shared borders have a variety of issues, ranging from substantial conflicts to relatively peaceful co-existence.

Pakistan

The border separating India and Pakistan is about 1,800 miles long. Both India and Pakistan were colonies of Britain, and when each country gained their independence, they subsequently went through a painful and extended partition where approximately 10 million people migrated. This border remains a highly contentious issue. Several such regions remain in dispute, have been the site of numerous military actions over the last few decades, and has threatened to re-ignite as recently as 2008. An article published by freelance author Kyle Mizokami, a defense writer located on the west coast of the US, pointed to the likelihood of a nuclear conflict with the most potential to escalate being between India and Pakistan, which are both nuclear nations[6]. This is a frightening thought in terms of the potential millions of people who would die indisputably, but also the overnight impact on our economic bonds with India and our own infrastructure. Ironically, it was China who instigated that India become a nuclear power, which is now the single biggest rival to Pakistan.

Bangladesh

The world's fifth-longest land border is the one shared by India and Bangladesh at 2,582 miles. The limit was decided after Bangladesh seceded from Pakistan. The most significant issue along the border is the constant smuggling mainly from India to Bangladesh. The Indian government initiated a shoot to kill policy to deter illegal immigrants from Bangladesh.

Nepal

The border between India and Nepal is approximately 1,092 miles long although the two countries have previously had issues on the exact position of the border. The Kali River was the source of the conflict, as neither country could agree on a precise demarcation. Efforts to resolve the issue have proved futile, as neither nation has ratified the border agreement. Recent incursions from China into this disputed area have heightened the tensions between the two rival nations with China using the lack of clarity on this border region as their invitation to inflame the issue. The potential for the escalation of conflict in this area is on the rise as China continues its expansion.

Sri Lanka

The shortest border between India and any nation is its 19-mile-long border with Sri Lanka. A series of treaties were signed and ratified by both nations between 1974 and 1976 to keep the border region safe. As the border is in the sea, the states have had issues with fishermen from one country fishing in the other country's territorial waters. Digging deeper into this border region, there are issues of health and HIV within the "boatmen" as a higher risk group due to their separation for extended periods of time from home, and social and family relationships.

Bhutan

The landlocked kingdom of Bhutan shares a 434-mile-long boundary with India. The border region has been relatively peaceful, as it is the only entry point on land for people and goods to travel to Bhutan due to the tension between China and Bhutan.

Afghanistan

India's 66-mile-long border with Afghanistan is not internationally recognized, as it is in the Kashmir region, which is currently under Pakistan's control. The Indian government continuously claims the territory as Indian land due to the historical ties.

The recent geo-political changes in Afghanistan due to the US' decision to unilaterally withdraw from the region significantly impacts India. This is due to India's contentious relationship with the Taliban, as well as India's on-going policy to counteract the Taliban's widening control on the country. India has substantial investment in infrastructure projects in Afghanistan within irrigation, hydroelectric, and industrial sectors. However, most significantly, India seeks to ensure that the Taliban does not act as a haven for terrorist training facilities and support like in the recent past. Nevertheless, as the saying goes, 'Afghanistan is the graveyard of empires', and it appears that it will keep its reputation intact, given their recent decisions.

My supposition is that Pakistan and Afghanistan will dramatically ramp up their efforts in Kashmir to completely unseat and further erode India's claims on that territory. Furthermore, this will exacerbate and escalate the conflict to a new level of urgency and warfare between India and Pakistan in the short term. It would be wise to understand this and monitor it closely for any potential spill over into other sections of India. This is especially important if China then decides to take advantage of the distraction to ramp up its conflicts and claims against other disputed border areas where India and China are engaged.

The recent withdrawal of US from Afghanistan has, in a way, significantly emboldened the Pakistan-based version of the Taliban. The Tahrik-e-Taliban operating in Pakistan has been invigorated by the success of its brother organization. They have begun to ramp up their efforts to destabilize sections of Pakistan with a significant potential to overflow into India along its substantial border.

There are a series of articles commenting on the Afghanistan and Pakistan's ability to destabilize the neighborhoods within India. A good launching site into these various articles can be found at Veteran Times (https://www.veteranstoday.com/2022/05/16/the-impact-of-afghanistans-insecurity-on-neighborhood-the-region-and-the-world/). The author, *Nazar Mohammad Mutmaeen, is a political analyst from this part of the world and writes on these geo-political topics. This article I have noted is May of 2022.*

China

India shares a 2,100-mile-long land border with China although control of two regions along the border is heavily contested by both countries, which eventually lead to a war in 1962. Despite numerous attempts to resolve the issue, both countries remain in a deadlock due to their military presence in the area. Incursions into the disputed areas, and the China policy of the String of Pearls are directly inflaming the tensions between these rival, nuclear nations.

The Indian Army has been undergoing a review for its readiness, especially in the eastern Ladakh where the risk of a Chinese incursion is greatest. As recently as October 2020, the defense minister, Rajnath Singh, met with the commanders in the region to review their readiness and ensure that all levels of preparedness are being considered and acted upon.

This ranges from road development and improvements to aid the movement of troops and materials to border vigilance and expected interference from the region's long-standing conflicts with insurgents within the border lands and forest regions in that area of India.

The current Map of Sino-Indian Border under the "Line of Actual Control"

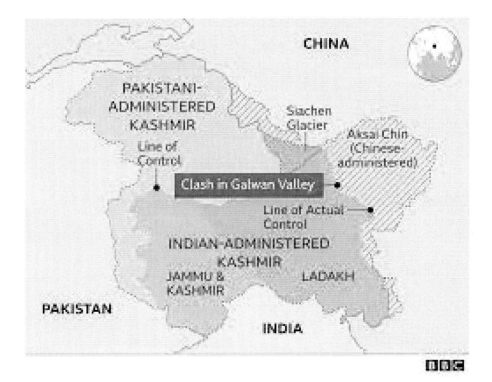

However, the death of Gen Bipin Rawat in December 2021, and India's failure to appoint a replacement for this top-level post thus far is of great concern, considering the readiness of the armed forces and the continuation of changes he had initiated. The Tribune has a good article concerning this gap in India's current leadership that is well worth the read (https://tribune.com.pk/story/2335302/loss-of-top-general-delaying-indias-military-reform-plans-say-experts).

It is a matter of trusting the person appointed to this post. Also, whether this powerful position can be trusted to act in India's best interest, considering the vast power in the consolidation of a bureaucratic 17-post system into a single office. As of now, there is no specific trust being found within the political establishment of India beyond the General's personal presence. The performance failures of the Indian Army in its limited war with Pakistan in 1999 question its ability to deal with a significant Chinese incursion, especially if it were coordinated with Pakistan to stress both borders simultaneously. The current statements of the defense minister on the army's readiness being excellent seems shallow and, at best, a bluster when put into perspective. Perhaps, the only saving grace for India from China's intentions now lie in Xi's consideration of which front he chooses to open: Taiwan or India.

Myanmar

India shares a 1,009-mile-long border with Myanmar across which India is constructing a barrier to reduce the influx of illegal goods from Myanmar. India and Myanmar have plans to join forces and establish a joint border patrol force to maintain security along the border. Recent issues in Myanmar within the conflicting ethnic groups have, as of yet, not spilled over into India, but attention is given to the potential for such an impact.

Pakistan and China pose specific external threats to India. Pakistan poses a threat due to the disputed territories and religious divisions since the 1947 partitioning of the post British colonies. Whereas, China, more recently, poses a significant threat primarily due to the expansionist economic goals of China. Another reason is because India is a regional threat both economically and as the only real military local threat, given the size of India's standing army and support from Western nations for arms and technological capabilities.

I have excluded any deep assessments of the military capabilities India and China. This is mostly because the topic would take me into an area I am not equipped to effectively communicate. Moreover, the topic in itself is capable of generating volumes of research and study well beyond this volume's purpose. However, I will state that the rivalry is very real. Further, India will likely not be capable of gaining the upper hand when it comes to competing with China, economically or militarily. Besides, India is likely the one with the most to lose as tensions for superiority intensifies and the rivalry expands. I believe control of the noose is in China's hands.

Terrorism in India

Here is a list of the active terroristic groups known to be operating in India.

- Indian Mujahedeen (IM)
- Hizb-ul-Mujahedeen
- Jammu and Kashmir Liberation Front
- Jamiat-ul-Mujahedeen
- Muslim Janbaz Force
- Tehrik-ul-Mujahedeen
- Lashkar-e-Jabbar
- Al Umar Mujahedeen
- Communist Party of India (Maoist)

As study published in April 2009 and used in an MBA prep study (https://testfunda.com/examprep) guide talks about the costs of terrorism in India, and it equates the losses to USD 32.7 Billion. There appears to be sufficient research behind this number to validate the value. Additionally, there is a stated death toll from loss of human capital of over 4,000. Indisputably, the real impact must include the loss of potential thought and future development: an impossible value to calculate but likely to be something substantial. However, it is safe to assume that innovation(s) and leadership is impacted whenever such a loss takes place. The latest data shows good news to some degree generally. Successful terrorist-driven attacks tended to be lower in 2019 with some minor exceptions in the Nagaland Maoist conflict area. While this can change any time, it is notable that the terrorist-related loss levels are the lowest since 1986. This sis mostly attributed to India's improvements in security measures according to the South Asia Intelligence Review portal https://www.satp.org/terrorism-assessment/india

Listed last among the terrorist organizations mentioned above is the Communist Party of India (Maoists). The list is not in order of their danger to the health of India or their future as a significant world power and economic force. In fact, the Naxalites of India are likely a more powerful eroding force in India than any of the external threats listed here. This internal threat has steadily grown in their ability to infiltrate and take control of substantial northern regional areas of India. This threat should not be underestimated, or else, the consequences are likely to be equal to or larger than the threat of China's expansionism at India's borders. These Maoist-trained and -focused forces can move about freely. They are likely already in the major urban areas critical to the outsourced facilities, operating in the streets and mingling about the human capital we depend on. It is highly likely that such forces are funded through underground systems that are beyond the current monitoring methods. One must ask ourselves who among those that harbor hostile intentions for India would want such an organized and funded campaign to be alive and well inside of India's own borders? Who would benefit most? Below is a statement from an early member of the Naxalitbari Marxist-Leninist system:

Without taking up the responsibility of organizing the class struggle, if you launch an armed struggle, it will inevitably become terrorism. It degenerated into a terrorist campaign. I've given it a name; it's an exercise in socialism in words, and terrorism in deeds," – Ashim Chatterjee, a member of the original Naxalbari uprising who now mediates between the government and the Maoists. (9 October 2015)

Chapter 7

The Healthcare System of India

Much like the issue of lack of security that is caused due to internal crime, inept police force, and military threats, healthcare is an infrastructure-based risk. The pandemic of 2019-2021 quickly revealed the cracks in the system around the world even in the highly developed "healthcare rich" nations like the US. India has a healthcare system that is a patchwork of marginally effective facilities to begin with. Such nations suffered from systematic conflicts of how best to organize a healthcare system that ranged from highly centralized, socialist styled, 'one size fits all' systems to highly privatized, for-profit, globally interacting, specialized care facilities and everything in between. The pitfalls include the following: an infrastructure that lacks coordinated care between locations; non-integrated systems and specialties with nonexistent records management; minimal distribution safeguards or methodologies; a governmental hodgepodge of ministries, bureaucracies, and centralized, regional, and local controlling agencies; a medical school system rife with inconsistencies; and nepotism-driven enrollment. It is a wonder that even aspirins are available, and in many of the outlying rural areas, even that is highly unlikely.

The attention and development of the medical vision and systems of India are driven by a 12-year plan that changes with the wind of the ruling party at the time it is created. Moreover, even when adopted, the funding of the core intentions and direction of the plan may or may not take place as evidenced in 2014. Thus, key agreements of what is needed are simply not funded, such that they fall away without any effort to implement. In some cases, "kitchen cabinet" activist groups, without any real authority, begin pushing for random, fractured, agenda items, thus resulting in squabbling and loss of focus. Simply put, healthcare in India is a mess. Should a pandemic arise targeting an even wider population than the Covid-19/21 SARS2 pandemic, I suspect millions would be lost in such an urban, intense, highly populated, and healthcare-sparse nation. For our purposes, a detail-rich volume by K. Sujatha Rao titled *"Do We Care? India's Health System"*, which is not a light read by any means, gives us a good background on understanding the complexity of the risk, and how the healthcare system of India can be a source of problems.

Below are some examples of how fractured the system is at the highest level of government.

"In 2014, the Union Health Secretary of the government of India was peremptorily transferred to another ministry. At the same year, the Cabinet Minister of Health was divested of his charge." (Rao 2017)

The report goes on to say that such administrative discretion was suspected of being influenced by an internal organization that did not support these individuals and sought to promote their own power while standing within the government.

In chapter 6 of Rao's study, she lists the key reasons for the conditions of failing healthcare industry in India. They are familiar themes to any human endeavor and why they fail: "Low funding priority for a particular purpose, weak governance, and an indifferent leadership."

Regardless of the foundational reasons for failures in this sector of India's governance, the fact remains that the quality and functional preparedness of the healthcare industry is less than marginal at best. They have achieved a high level of profitable medical advances and success for esoteric and primarily foreign participation such as inexpensive plastic surgery, dental improvements, and low-cost, "resort-style," medical vacationing. However, the failure of their healthcare sector is because they have achieved little in terms of the following: rural healthcare accessibility; gains against stunted growth syndrome among the poorer populations; access to preventative healthcare for majority of its population; improvement and civilian participation in pre-natal and post-natal care; integration of records management across the spectrum of healthcare centers; and implementation of new technology within its regional- and state-run hospitals and medical clinics. Simply put, programs come and go with funding. The later lack of funding, priority changes, and shifts in public policy leave improvements and "righting wrongs" dangling in the wind. For example, the Pradhan Mantri National Dialysis Program, which achieved legislative relief allowing by passing "made in India" demands machinery that is available for use, distribution, and purchase with federal dollars allowable with marginal and limited implementation. How does one deploy such technology to a hospital of 8 beds that does not have the ability to support, use, and be maintained in a remote and underserved area? A typical case of governmental failure: tying 200 yards of line on a lifebuoy and throwing it 400 yards over the heads of those who need it; or, conversely, tying 50 yards of line, throwing it short, and telling the drowning subject to swim for it; either way, the person drowns. It is no wonder that India is the 3rd worldwide in underweight children: a malady that creates a lifelong disability in terms of physical and mental growth for the child, thus limiting their ability to compete long-term, and by direct result, dragging down the nation's future, expected abilities[16]. Studying the hard data of India in terms of healthcare practitioners, we see the numbers begin to tell us a story of how India is building its infrastructure to care for its citizens. Table 1 shows the comparisons as a point of reference.

The unsettled battle between federalism and centralized national control for the healthcare economic sectors continue to teeter back and forth with no clear resolution. In an effort to sort this out, in 2016, this matter was pushed forward without much thought of how the new responsibility would be picked up and funded within the state. Undoubtedly, the result was a highly ineffective transition with minimal planning. Unsurprisingly, such a governance failure failed to produce any significant positive results. This issue goes to the very heart of the definition of the lack of governance mentioned above.

India has an additional layer of hurdles to overcome in this sector of risk as they attempt to improve their primary care system. I will use Rao's term here, "peripatetic quackery," especially within its less educated and isolated rural populations. However, this is not the only group to fall to such "healthcare" methods, given the depth of India's ritualistic and religiously guided population. During the early height of the 2019-2021 Covid-19 Pandemic, hanging a specific, badge-like device called "The Anti-Virus Lock Out Badge" around one's neck was believed to ward off the virus. Several thousands were sold to primarily urban, highly educated parts of the population. Most of Asia banned these devices and labeled them a complete scam. However, I cannot find such an article where India joined the ban or made such a statement to dissuade their sale and use as a protection against Covid-19. There could have been one, but my searches in the various official news outlets like the Times of India, Orange 9, etc. came back without any findings.

An important consideration when discussing the health care of India is that they are at a "Very High Risk" for infectious diseases, given the level of care available, density of population, and level of poverty, all while noting the lack of sanitation and access to clean water sources for large segments of the population. For example, reports for a highly contagious and deadly disease called Nipah Virus recently appeared in the local news reports. Such conditions can easily develop and rage through these communities. While it may not become a pandemic issue, it certainly has the potential to become epidemic within the nation or, at a minimum, the local urban areas.

New Delhi, September 5, 2021—Authorities in India's southern Kerala state are racing to contain an outbreak of the Nipah virus. The virus, which is not related to the coronavirus behind the current global pandemic, but is far more deadly, killed a 12-year-old boy in Kerala over the weekend, prompting stepped-up efforts to trace his contacts. New infections have been confirmed.

The boy was admitted to a hospital a week ago with high fever. As his condition worsened and doctors suspected inflammation of his brain (encephalitis), his blood samples were sent to the National Institute of Virology, where tests confirmed a Nipah infection. He died early on Sunday.

Government authorities have stepped up contact tracing efforts, identifying, quarantining, and testing people who may have come into contact with the young victim. According to the state's health minister, Veena George, 188 people who came into contact with the boy had been identified by Monday. Of them, 20 were considered high-risk primary contacts — primarily his family members, all of whom were being held under strict quarantine or hospitalized.[12]

The Top Ten Causes of Death in India

1. Heart disease
2. Chronic obstructive pulmonary disease (COPD)
3. Stroke
4. Diarrheal diseases
5. Lower respiratory infection
6. Tuberculosis
7. Neonatal disorders
8. Asthma
9. Diabetes
10. Chronic kidney disease

The US CDC works with the Government of India on several initiatives assisting them in building response teams for disasters, infectious disease outbreaks and tracking, training, records keeping, and systems that support information sharing, etc.

Endemic Diseases in India

At least 14 endemic diseases
already prevalent in India

DISEASE	CAUSE	
Dengue	Virus	
Chikungunya	Virus	
Echinococcosis	Tapeworm	
Kala-azar	Protozoa	
Leprosy	Bacteria	
Soil-transmitted helminthiases	Worm	
Taeniasis/cysticercosis	Tapeworm	
Trachoma	Bacteria	
Foodborne trematodiases	Flatworm	
Lymphatic filariasis	Worm	
Rabies	Virus	
Snakebite	Venom	
Mycetoma	Bacteria	
Scabies	Mites	

Source: World Health Organisation

DW

The Health Ministry of India has now declared the latest outbreak of SARS (Sars2), commonly referred to as Covid 19, as being endemic to India. According to World Health Organization (WHO) and Indian health spokespeople, COVID-19 is entering the endemic stage:

The World Health Organization (WHO) chief scientist, Soumya Swaminathan, recently stated that India is at or approaching the endemic stage. She, while cautioning that things can change unexpectedly in a pandemic, specified that the country will still keep noticing small outbreaks in a few parts where the vaccine coverage is low. Swaminathan also pointed out a mass blood sampling study that showed 65% seroprevalence for coronavirus in Indians. Seroprevalence represents the level of antibodies in the population of a particular country. (Nov 2021/ https://pharmeasy.in/blog/is-india-entering-the-stage-of-endemic-what-does-it-mean/)

Recently, the Health Ministry of India made the following statement as well:

NEW DELHI: Covid-19 is already in an endemic stage in India; NEW DELHI: Covid-19 is already in an endemic stage in India. According to Dr. Gangandeep Kang in Delhi, COVID-19 is already endemic in India per a report in the Times of India Feb 14, 2022: https://timesofindia.indiatimes.com/india/explained-is-covid-in-india-in-endemic-stage/articleshow/89567924.cms

An article that I had read in Scientific American, dated early 1980's, predicted the occurrence of other pandemics. I am unable to cite the exact article at this point. However, it easily foretold that, given our ability to put a large number of people into a flying tube and disembark those people from nearly any point on earth, regardless of how remote and uninhabited, to any other point on earth within 24 hours, we will also inevitably transport and disembark any number of bacteria and viruses willingly or otherwise along with us. The lack of a mechanism to detect and isolate incoming 'uninvited guests' as we travel from point to point is part of the environment we now live in and have been living for some time. Perhaps, we have been incredibly lucky up until this point, as pandemics are still a rare event.

Chapter 8

Social Upheaval

Let us start with a list of the social conditions that lead to upheaval and social conflict. India's list is not unique. Except a few areas, this list could be applied to many nations on Earth to one degree or another. In the western democracies, we like to think that we have dealt with these issues and have put them behind us. In some cases, this is true. I will not debate the severity of these issues within the western democracies in an us vs. them manner. The fact is that extremes and purists on all sides will come to this topic with their own agendas and perceptions. I can neither solve it nor suggest solutions, as it is far outside the purpose of this book. I will only say that no nation on Earth is a utopian society. It is an ongoing struggle for us all.

That said, below is a list of social struggles within India. Some of these may pertain to our work within India, and some, although part of the landscape, do not directly impact our work.

1. Caste system
2. Poverty
3. Child labor
4. Gender Inequality at work
5. Illiteracy
6. Low status of women

7. Child marriage

8. Dowry system

9. Sati practice

10. Alcoholism

11. Superstition

12. Sanitation and cleanliness

13. Religious conflicts

14. Beggary

15. Juvenile delinquency

1. Caste System

Simply put, it is an assignment to a social level by birth, and it dictates one's profession/work, likely one's housing and physical location, and level of earning potential. It is arguably the same in most nations, but without the severe stigmas the system can impose to the point of being an "untouchable". The Indian government has enacted various laws and practices in more recent times to end this system with some marginal successes. One such practice involves holding "n" number of elected representative seats in government to the "Sudra" class, while another is the deinstitutionalization of the term "Untouchable". However, there are still positions and social placements where only the "untouchable" class can apply and escaping such a social place is highly unlikely.

Except for the famers uprising in 2020, India tends to be socially quite stable. However, there are deep underlying issues that will not go away and will eventually boil up in some unexpected but likely violent ways. Poverty is rampant and affects large segments of the society. In the past, multiple famines have happened in India where many millions of people died. I suspect that, should another significant famine take place, which appears to be likely, given Indian's cyclical history of famine, it will kick start a violent response. Such a response would not have been seen in earlier times due to the heavy hand of the British Empire sitting on top of those events over the last two centuries. This is no longer the case, and nor is the political world same as it was during that time when putting down a rebellion was a standard fare for the colonizing nations.

Rampant poverty, however, of so many people, considering India's population, can certainly generate mass movements we have not encountered in the past. Such conditions, coupled with a severe food shortage, could easily be a lit fuse to ignite a critical event. India has not resolved the impact of its poverty in many parts of the nation. Illiteracy and failed school systems are common with only marginal. The India-Bangladesh borders virtually have cities of bordellos where women are born into the trade as part of generational social conditions and physical location. With the expected health issues associated with such conditions, the highly transient workers moving between the two nations are both infecting the sex workers and being infected by the sex workers. An excellent resource, among the numerous other studies available, is a study from Ambarish Kumar Rai, "Nature of sex trafficking in India: A geographical perspective" with an article published in January 2021 https://www.sciencedirect.com/science/article/abs/pii/S0190740920321629. I have also listed several books in the bibliography that are specific to the social conditions in India.

2. Poverty

Getting reliable information concerning poverty in India is very difficult. Research will show stark contrasts: everything from glowing reports on how well the government has done to lift people out of poverty due to the rising economic fortunes of the nation to a large percentage still trapped in poverty due to a wide list of reasons including corruption, climate change, lack of education, etc. This results from skimming only for what is needed and ignoring whatever does not fit into our narrative. Suffice it to say that India's poverty will not be solved by a few outsourcing contracts. However, we can ameliorate some of its impact by providing decent wages to those who have secured an education and worked to take part in the growing success of the nation. Despite the successes and opportunities, we must understand that many parts of India are in a cycle of extreme poverty for whatever reason and that as the population continues to expand, there are simply not enough opportunities to overcome all the reasons for India's poverty. A quick review of the World Economic Forum and World Bank mentions some of the brighter points. The challenge of population growth and the disparities between India's rural and urban populations will be ongoing issues for the foreseeable future. I believe it would be a good idea for our contracts to include a commitment to some organization that is working with the rural poor of India in some area such as health care, education, food distribution, etc. A small percentage could be directed to such organizations to recognize the disparity, and, at a minimum, make some financial accounting of that recognition. Having our outsourcing partner make such a commitment in contract is something we can easily add to the price of the work.

Here is a link to a very comprehensive InfoGraphic of the poverty in India by various categories; age, location, education, industry, sex, etc.: https://www.worldbank.org/en/news/infographic/2016/05/27/india-s-poverty-profile. I have copied a picture of the graphic into the appendix.

Many of the ills within the society of India are not unique to them and tracking them individually as risks does not make sense for this books purpose. With the exception of how we pay and treat the women within our teams, our direct involvement with these ills is outside of our control or ability to address. As mentioned, it is wise to be aware and mindful that these conditions exist, and they can change for better or for worse as time goes. Pay attention to those events, which could impact our work and the teams we employ. The two areas we do have direct control over are the way in which we treat and compensate the women on our teams. I hope that you take advantage of the best practices possible in this segment of our employment.

The appendix of this book has a list of the charities working in the various sectors within India. You may choose to become a contributor as part of your personal life or, perhaps, involve your company as part of social responsibility adding value to the partnership.

3. Child Labor

Fortunately, child labor is a highly unlikely to be an issue the world of outsourcing must deal with. Obviously, we should guard against any such encroachment of this societal ill into our industry but the very nature of the work we do makes this an unlikely matter for us to deal with.

4. Gender Inequality at Work

This issue is something we can impact if we are operating in India with our outsource team or directly. Many of your team members will be women and they will often be very skilled and valuable members of your team. Make it clear to your team leaders you expect every member, regardless of gender, to be compensated and treated with the same level of respect and given the same level of opportunity to grow, advance and contribute as every other member of the team.

5. 15 Other Societal Ills

The remaining Social Ills in the list above are something to be aware either impact or the likelihood of encountering is unlikely. I list them here only because they do exist in India but so it is good to be aware of them as good and informed citizens.

Without being insensitive to the cruelty that some of these issues impart on the Indian society, I feel they are neither impactful nor due to any direct fault of the economics of outsourcing or the high-tech industry within India. As stated, I have added an index of charitable organizations operating within India, which you may want to be aware of and supportive of.

Chapter 9

Civil Infrastructure

Civil infrastructure is a critical element that needs to be understood and closely tracked. I have broken this area into several segments as follows:

1. Power and Energy Stability

2. Domestic Transport and International Accessibility – Intermodal

3. Health Systems

4. Educational Systems

5. Water/Sanitation

6. Environmental Compliance

7. Political Stability

8. Public Safety and Security Stability

9. Interconnectivity

10. Banking (BIC/SWIFT)

    a. https://bicswift.org

11. Intercontinental cable connectivity

    a. https://www.submarinecablemap.com

These components directly impact the stability and operational success of your outsourcing arrangement. Thus, tracking them crucial for your risk management strategy.

1. Power and Energy Stability

As we are aware, access to fuel has been very much in the news. India has secured oil from Russia despite the world's current stand to isolate and punish Russia for its invasion of Ukraine. India has stood firm saying that it has an obligation to its nation and its people for their continued economic life. It is hard to argue with that logic and to, at least, acknowledge the truth in that policy. The fact remains that India, like other nations with expanding economies, is struggling to sustain economic growth, all the while attempting to reduce their impact on the environment and reliance on "non-green" production methods to generate that growing energy need. Reportedly, India will need to double its energy production in the next decade to maintain its growth curve. In October 2021, the Ministry of Energy issued a set of rules and changes to its earlier policy to find a balance between the power plants deemed as "must-run" locations, kilowatt hours it must produce to maintain economic growth, and the commitments made to reduce greenhouse gases. This is a daunting undertaking to balance these demands. 2030 is a landmark point and tracking India's ability to sustain its 2021 policy decisions is a critical component to monitor, as this metric will most certainly directly impact India's ability to provide quality support.

2. Domestic Transport and International Accessibility – Intermodal

In 2018, Amit Kumar Ghosh, Joint Secretary of Ministry of Road Transport and Highways, presented a plan and situation for India's roadway and intermodal development. The report appears to be quite open in terms of successes and failures/matters for improvement. In terms of the risks to a system implemented and supported at a site in India, this is not a critical item. This conclusion is drawn assuming that the system implementation will take some time to be put in place and that it will be scheduled as a one-time event with, perhaps, some additional components being added from occasionally to account for the updates and replacements over time. However, it does indicate that a good plan will include the localized storage of spare parts and common failure items paying close attention to Mean Time Between Failure (MTBF) of various components and technological updates. Generally, the sites are accessible, and intermodal issues are of low impact in this industry. A copy of Mr. Ghosh's presentation can be located here for greater detail: https://www.unescap.org/sites/default/files/India_CBStrengthening%20Transport_March_0.pdf

3. Health Systems

The health systems in India have been covered in Chapter 6. This area has challenges that can impact your team members, thus, it is worth observing. Moreover, understanding that the effectiveness of healthcare in India is not a given, we must ensure that our team bench is prepared for changes, and extended absences is an item that must be monitored on a regular basis.

4. Educational Systems

Ironically the importance and demand for education as a core social norm in India belies some of the realities of the poor in the rural and urban centers of India. Furthermore, this issue directly impacts your team and its future capabilities. It is an

85

area in which you are either a direct beneficiary or a victim of its failures, but you have limited direct input to this. It is a risk with a direct mitigating strategy. You can establish a means to monitor your freshers, a rising critical team member, and the one to likely leave a new open seat soon. Maintain the skill's matrix and ensure it is closely monitored. You may want to possess and method that allows you to donate toward skills development, but do so with caution, as you do not want to place skill development.

5. Water/Sanitation

Surprisingly, numerous excellent books written on this topic were interesting and entertaining. They provided a view into the aspects of Indian history and culture not found in most readings about the nation and its people. I was especially fascinated by the economics involved in the sanitation side of this topic. In it, open air, a still preferred method for sanitation in the some more isolated rural sectors of India, is preferred and considered an environmentally friendlier way to deal with human waste. Another interesting component of the topic was the legacy rights to muck out private septic systems, and the generational passage of those rights within families for the right to the materials from the activity for their agricultural or commercial use. These rights are closely guarded and are a culturally protected part of the rural poor's almost medieval mechanisms for dealing with what we in the industrialized world would consider a simple "flush and forget" part of our daily lives.

The bottom line was the national lack of clean water systems and sanitation. As India entered the 1980's, there was a great deal of effort put into clean water and sanitation systems in the major urban centers. Many of the under-street pipes had been laid by the same British who had ties to the old-world London systems flowing out to the Thames. Opening the streets and examining the pipes, which was a precarious work at best, revealed a massive maze of unmarked pipes that could be clean water or sewerage. The major urban areas have largely improved this issue over the last two decades, but as a nation, there is still much to be done including introducing the benefits of using toilets as opposed to open fields for many of the rural population.

However, a discussion of waste in India goes beyond human waste and clean water. A simple example is the need to institute recycling of the growing accumulation of commercial packaging for goods consumed by a population of several millions. For instance, the use of toothpaste. We barely think about such a commodity, but in India, it has a very real impact on their ability to digest its introduction into daily life. In the US, we use the product almost universally. The used-up toothpaste tube gets tossed into the waste basket and eventually discarded with whatever local method used for taking away such consumer packaging, along with all of the other packages tossed out that week. In India, such packaging has nowhere to go, and efforts to introduce recycling systems, portable small systems, collection centers, special programs to establish workable recycling efforts, etc. have had very limited success in getting a foothold. Imagine the tonnage of waste created by just the toothpaste tubes in the three cities studied here with populations growing annually between 3 to 5 % starting at approximately 38,000,000 in 2022. The significance of the challenge is staggering, and when taken nationally for billions of people, it must seem insurmountable.

6. Environmental Compliance

As we all know, some form of compliance mandate will eventually come into play reaching all levels of the waste we produce through human activities. For it to be enforceable, it will have some form of financial cost/reward formula. Could it reach into our contractual arrangements for the vendors we select, and how their compliance gets measured and enforced? Most likely yes. I think of the tax codes and compliance to the US laws for how we deal with the foreign corruption prevention laws as a for instance. As of now, I do not see how India can comply with any such environmental compliance agreement, as they simply do not have the systems in place to comply, and they are a signatory to various UN International agreements of environmental protections. Although at this point, there are limited mechanisms for enforcement with any teeth, those teeth are coming. Can your outsourcer meet the conditions you may need to enact contractually?

7. Political Stability

Prime Minister Narendra Modi on Thursday asserted that India is a country of political stability and policy continuity with a commitment to democracy and diversity. Delivering a special keynote address at the US-India Strategic Partnership Forum's 3rd Annual Leadership Summit, the PM highlighted that India has undertaken far-reaching reforms to make business easier and red-tapism lesser.

The following excerpt is from a statement reported by Zee Media on Sep 03, 2020:

Despite our large local needs, we did not shy away from our global responsibilities. We supplied generic medicines to the world. We are also at the forefront of vaccine research. You have a govt. that believes in delivering results, and you are looking at a country with political stability and policy continuity commitment in democracy and diversity," he said.

He stated that for challenges in India, "you have a government that believes in delivering results," for which ease of living is as important as ease of doing business. "You are looking at a young country with 65 per cent population less than 35 years old," said PM Modi. The PM said that India is becoming a major attraction for foreign investments adding that "we have received USD 20 billion in foreign investment in 2020.

There is no reason to doubt the comment, and most Indians and other nations have not said anything to contrary. Of course, there are political spats and hyperboles to be expected within any governmental body where one party, group, or another has disparaging things to say from their perspective and if their ox is being gored or not. However, I would add a cautionary note that some of the issues India is dealing with internally and internationally, especially the challenges with Pakistan and China that are supported by direct incursions or terroristic means are significant enough to be vigilant of. This metric is something to monitor.

An article in "Dissent Magazine" refers to a paper written by Myron Weiner and Bert F. Hoselitz in the early 1960's that talks about economic development as a baseline defense against political instability. It is still true today and is a quick read

(https://www.dissentmagazine.org/article/india-economic-development-and-political-stability-in-india).

8. Public Safety and Security Stability

The earlier chapters have covered this aspect of risk including external threats and the statistics of the lack of a coherent and nationwide policing system. It is worth monitoring and belongs in a discussion of risks.

9. Interconnectivity

Interconnectivity refers to two significant risk areas to monitor. The first is the banking system formerly known as "SWIFT" and recently rebranded as "BIC". These are Level 1 and Level 2 network monitoring areas that are likely a part of your ongoing monitoring systems within your network /IT team's purview. Maintaining these reporting statistics and warning systems should include both the internet connectivity channels we use through a variety of systems as vital KPI/SLA metrics. Lack of Redundancy can be a significant risk as well and is a critical component for these systems.

10. Cable companies in India with landing sites in the referenced table.

Landing site ownership into India

Currently, there are 15 subsea cables (17 if SEACOM and MENA are considered separate cables) landing in 15 cable landing stations in 5 cities across India in Mumbai, Chennai, Cochin, Tuticorin, and Trivandrum.

BSNL plans to construct new cable landing stations in Digha, Cochin, and the Andaman & Nicobar Islands. IOx will construct a new cable landing station at Puducherry. Reliance Jio is planning for new cables and landing stations.

- Tata Communications owns five cable landing stations: three in Mumbai, and one each in Chennai and Cochin.

- Global Cloud Xchange, formerly Reliance Globalcom, owns the Versova Cable Landing Station in Mumbai for FALCON, and Trivandrum cable landing station for WARF cable connecting Maldives and Sri Lanka to India.

- Reliance Jio owns <u>BBG cable landing station in Chennai,</u> and <u>AAE-1 cable landing station at Versova beach in Mumbai.</u>

- Bharti Airtel owns three cables landing stations: two in <u>Chennai</u> and one in <u>Mumbai.</u>

- Sify Technologies owns <u>cable landing station in Mumbai</u> for <u>MENA,</u> and <u>GBI</u> submarine cable systems.

- BSNL owns its first international submarine cable connecting India and Sri Lanka (<u>BLCS</u>), and its <u>cable landing station in Tuticorin.</u> The <u>Digha Cable Landing Station</u> in West Bengal was newly approved in May 2011 by the Department of Telecommunication (DoT) of India for a submarine cable project between India and South-east Asia. BNSL is expected to own the <u>Digha Cable Landing Station.</u> BSNL has chosen NEC to build the <u>Chennai-Andaman & Nicobar Islands (A&N Islands) submarine cable system,</u> constructing a new cable landing station in Chennai and several stations in the <u>Andaman & Nicobar Islands.</u>

- Vodafone owns <u>BBG cable landing station in Mumbai.</u>

- IOx plans to construct a new cable landing station at Puducherry for its <u>IOx cable.</u>

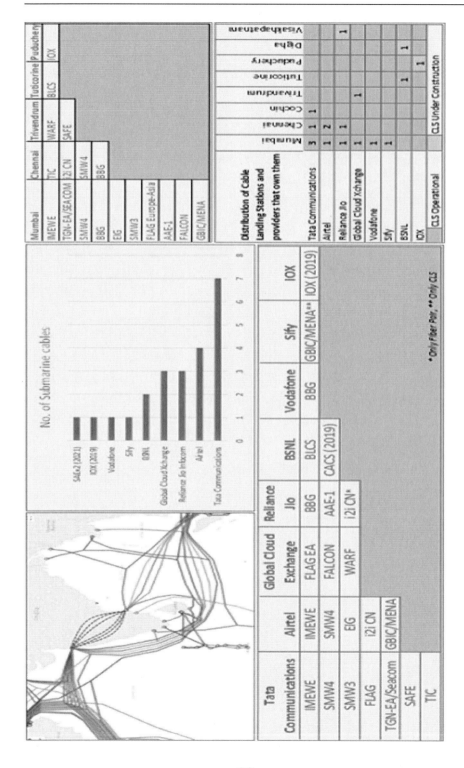

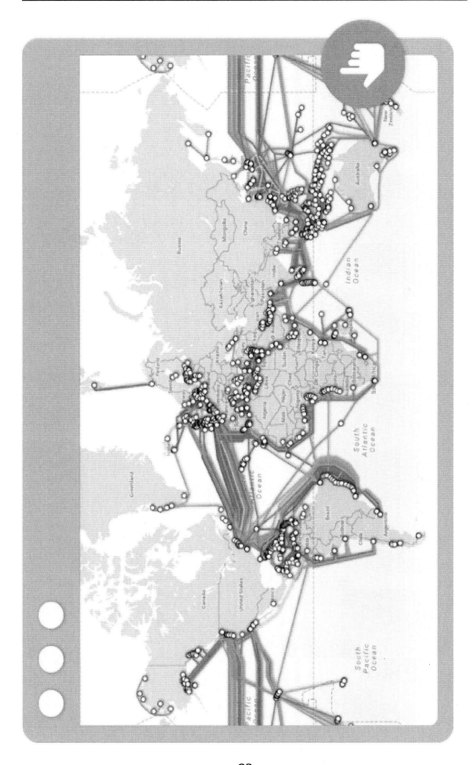

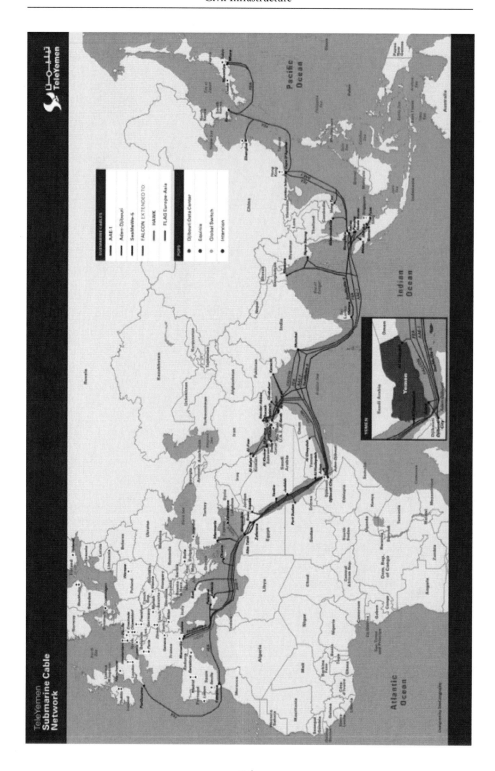

Comparative Data India & Other Technological Nations

*USA Literacy Rates are calculated under specific standards requiring respondents to take part in PIAAC testing. The actual overall literacy at a minimal level of competency is 85% of all 16+ participants.
Rankings are quoted from either the CIA World Fact Book or WHO Nation Rankings where statistics do not exist in one or the other, as both are credible resource reference documents in the author's opinion.
This list of nations has been picked due to their level of investment in terms of dollars, their hiring/attracting talent, and strength of their AI/Machine learning position when measured globally. The assumption is that if AI/Machine Learning is to be a significant driver of future technological advancement, then selecting an outsourcing team that is outside this list is going to be a liability in the near future.
AI data is difficult to summarize, given a wide variety of sources reporting on this topic. I have selected this source, as it is relevant and a more concise list based on measurable data (https://www.analyticsinsight.net/top-10-countries-leading-the-artificial-intelligence-race/,
https://worldpopulationreview.com/country-rankings/literacy-rate-by-country).
CIA World Fact Book Source of Data

WHO Country Detail Report

NR = Not Reported

Table 1a Tick Tock India

Rank by Tortoise Index of Technology Leadership	In Order of AI Investment — Rank by Investment in AI/Machine Learning and Talent Acquisition	General Healthcare National Data		
		Significant Healthcare Metrics for general population		
		% Expenditure on Healthcare	Physicians /1000	Hospital beds/1000	Risk Factor Major Infectious Disease
US	China	5.4	1.98	4.3	High
China	USA*	16.9	2.61	2.4	Low
UK	UK	10	2.81	2.5	Low
Canada	Canada	10.8	2.31	2.5	Low
Israel		7.5	4.63	3	Low
	Russia	5.3	3.75	8.1	Medium
Germany	Australia	9.3	3.68	3.8	Low
Netherlands		10	3.61	3.3	Low
	Germany	11.4	4.25	8	Low
	Norway	10.1	2.92	3.6	Low
South Korea		7.6	2.36	12.3	Low
	Sweden	10.9	3.98	2.2	Low
Singapore		4.5	2.29	2.5	Low
France	France	11.3	3.27	6	Low
	India	3.5	0.86	0.5	Very High
Finland		9	3.81	3.3	Low
Ireland		6.9	3.31	3	Low

Chile has also placed a significant investment in attaining a viable presence in AI/Machine Learning in their future and is well-worth watching as they further develop this capability. I have not pulled their data here, but it is available in these mentioned resource documents.

Chilean Statement on Digital Future and governmental commitment: https://read.oecd-ilibrary.org/governance/digital-government-in-chile-a-strategy-to-enable-digital-transformation_3e74cf50-en#page1

Table 1b Tick Tock India

| | Environmental Metrics | | | | | | | | | | | | |
| | Significant Environmental Pollutant Metrics | | | Solid Waste Annual Creation Million Tonnage | | | Resource Management Metrics | | | % Access to Improved Water Source | | % Access to Sanitation Facilities | |
	CO2 Megatons	Particulant Matter Micrograms/Ft3	Methane Emissions Megatons	Created	Recycled	Recycle %	Renewable Water Resources Billion Cubic Meters	Total Water Withdrawal Muni, Indust & Agro Bil Cubic Meters	Water Use Against Annual Reserve	Rural	Urban	Rural	Urban
	9893.04	49.16	1490.24	210	unreported		2.84E+12	5.98E+11	21%	87.80	97.70	82.00	97.00
	5006.3	7.4	685.4	258	89.3	0.3461	3.069E+12	5.88E+10	2%	97.00	100.00	100.00	100.00
	379.02	10.53	49.16	31.567	8.6	0.2724	1.470E+11	7.51E+09	5%	100.00	100.00	100.00	100.00
	544.89	6.48	101.82	25.1	5.2	0.2072	3.E+12	3.56E+01	0.00%	98.90	100.00	98.70	100.00
	65.17	19.46	13.02	5.4	1.35	0.25	1.78E+11	2.30E+09	1.29%	100	100	100	100
	1732.03	13.75	851.52	60	2.7	0.045	4.53E+12	6.44E+10	1%	94.20	98.60	78.10	94.80
	375.91	7.19	105.01	13.345	5.618	0.421	4.92E+11	1.66E+10	3%	100.00	100.00	100.00	100.00
	170.78	12.07	17.79	8.855	2.179	0.2461	9.10E+10	1.61E+10	17.67%	100.00	100.00	100.00	100.00
	727.97	11.71	49.92	51.046	24.4	0.478	1.540E+11	2.44E+10	16%	100.00	100.00	100.00	100.00
	41.02	7.02	4.81	2.187	0.572	0.2615	3.93E+11	2.69E+09	1%	100.00	100.00	100.00	100.00
	620.3	24.57	30.28	18.219	10.567	0.58	6.97E+11	2.71E+10	4%	100.00	100.00	100.00	100.00
	43.25	5.89	4.42	4.377	1.417	0.3237	1.740E+11	2.38E+00	0%	100.00	100.00	100.00	100.00
	37.54	18.26	4.4	7.70	4.70	0.6104	6.000E+08	6.59E+08	110%	100.00	100.00	100.00	100.00
	Not Reported	11.64	55.99	33.339	7.435	0.223	2.110E+11	2.64E+10	13%	100.00	100.00	100.00	100.00
	2,407.67	65.2	559.11	168.4	8.42	0.05	1.91E+12	7.61E+11	40%	91.00	96.00	61.10	93.70
	45.87	5.88	4.46	2.738	0.77	0.2812	1.1E+11	1.867E+12	17%	100.00	100.00	100.00	100.00
	37.71	51	13.67	2.693	0.889	0.3301	5.20E+10	8.61E+08	2%	98.10	97.00	99.00	97.70

Table 1c Tick Tock India

General Population Data						
Literacy Total Population	Infant Mortality Rate/1000	Infant mortality Rank	Children Underweight & World Position		Population Obesity and world rank	
			Country	World Rank	Percent Obese	World rank
96%	11.15	169	2.4	103	6.2	169
99%	5.22	176	0.4	130	36.2	12
99%	3.68	186	NR	148	27.8	36
99%	4.4	184	NR	NA	29.4	26
97.8%	3.62	195	NR	NA	26.1	44
99%	6.51	169	NR	NA	23.1	70
99%	3.05	214	0.550	136	29	27
99%	3.45	201	NR	NA	20.4	99
99%	3.24	208	0.500	127	22.3	79
100%	2.34	220	NR	NR	23.1	68
99%	2.9	215	0.070	NR	4.7	184
100%	2.45	218	NR	NR	20.6	97
99%	1.56	226	NR	NR	6.1	171
99%	3.19	209	NR	NR	21.6	87
74.4%	39.55	40	33.400	3	3.9	189
99%	2.15	222	NR	NR	22.2	80
99%	3.52	197	NR	NR	25.3	51

List of Charitable Organizations Operating within India

India has a long history of being a charitable society. Charity is a tradition within the culture of supporting those in need from child hunger, health, and education to supporting the elderly and everything between. This includes the nation's indigenous animal populations and those impacted by disasters and calamities.

It is up to you to determine which of these organizations, if any, you wish to contribute to, undoubtedly considering your company's policies for such actions and whether these organizations meet the standards of the US Treasury Department to qualify as 501 C (3) deductible contributions.

With several organizations in India, selecting one, if you so choose, will be a difficult task. I have listed a few that, at least at the time of publication of this book, appear to be doing good and successful work and would be somewhat related to the needs of an outsourcing arrangement. Two on the list are something we would not likely think about, especially in the western nations. The first of these is LEPRA, an NGO that works with those suffering from leprosy. Leprosy is truly something that is all but forgotten to ancient history by those of us in the west. However, in India, it is still very much a reality in some sections of the country. The second is directed to the older generation. India does not have the social net we have in the west, so the elderly is often in extreme poverty and deep hunger.

This is a very thin list of the available NGOs and charitable organizations throughout India. Perhaps, just mentioning this idea here as part of your contracting efforts will stimulate some of my readers to consider making this part of your arrangement as you move to select and contract with your outsourcer. Obviously, if not India, I am sure there are many other people and locations that could benefit from your presence with this concept.

https://www.usaid.gov/india/water-and-sanitation

https://www.pratham.org/

https://www.sightsaversindia.in/

https://www.cry.org/

https://goonj.org/

https://www.nanhikali.org/

https://leprasociety.in/

https://sammanfoundation.org/

https://www.smilefoundationindia.org/

https://www.helpageindia.org/

https://www.akshayapatra.org/

Tick Tock India Bibliography and References

Balslev, A.N (Editor) (2013). On India, Self-Image and Counter Image. New Delhi India, Sage Publications

Bhatnagar, Zubin (2019). Strategic Stability in South Asia, Challenges, and Implications for India. New Delhi, Vij Books India Pvt Ltd

Chatterjee, Kingshuk, Editor (2013): Pakistan and Afghanistan, The (in)Stability Factor in India's Neighborhood. New Delhi. KW Private Ltd

Coffee D. and Spears D. (2017): Where India Goes, Abandoned Toilets, Stunted Development, and the Costs of Caste. Uttar Pradesh India. Harper Collins

Dahiya, R. – Behuria, A.K. Editors (2012): India's Neighborhood, Challenges in the Next Two Decades. New Delhi: Institute for Defense Studies and Analysis

Doran A and Jeffrey R. (2018): Waste of a Nation, Garbage and Growth in India: Cambridge USA & London UK. Harvard Press

Engerman, D.P. (2020). The Price of Aid in India, Cambridge USA, Harvard Press

Gardner, K. (Editor) (2021) The Frontier Complex: Geopolitics and the Making of the India-China Border, 1846–1962. London. Cambridge University Press

Gera, Y.K. (Maj Gen, Retd), Editor (2019): Asia Pacific Region, Assessment of the Security Architecture. New Delhi. Vij Books of India Pvt. Ltd

Gupta, C. (2001). Sexuality-Obscenity-Community, Women, Muslims and the Hindu Public in Colonial India. New York, Palgrave

Infrastructure Development Finance Company (2021). Infrastructure Development Finance Company Report. Mumbai India, IDFC Press

Jayaraman, G. (2017). Who Me, Poor? How India's Youth are Living in Urban Poverty. Delhi: Bloomsbury

Johny, S. (Editor) (2019). McMahon Line, The, A Century of Discord, A Review. New Delhi, Bloomsbury

Naisbitt, J. (1996). Megatrends In Asia. Eight Asian Megatrends the are Reshaping Our World. New York, Simon and Shuster

Noorani, A.G. (2011): India–China Boundary Problem 1846–1947: History and Diplomacy. London. Oxford Press

Rao, K.S. (2017). Do We Care? India's Health System. New Delhi, Oxford Press

Shah, S.P. (2014). Street Corner Secrets, Sex, Work and Migration in the City of Mumbai. Durham USA, Duke Univ Press

Sharma, Dr R.S. (2009). Cratons and Fold Belts of India. Berlin-London-New York, Springer

Singh, J.J. (Author) (2019) The Frontier Complex: Geopolitics and the Making of the India-China Border, 1846–1962, India. Harper Collins

Vivekananda, Swami (1954). To the Youth of India. Kolkata India, Advaita Ashram

Vohra, N.N. (2016). Safeguarding India, Essays on Governance and Security. Uttar Pradesh India, Harper Collins

Internet Articles, Books and Resource Items

Central Intelligence Agency, (2021). World Fact Book. Washington DC, US Gov Printing Office

https://www.cia.gov/the-world-factbook/countries/india/

New India Express.com (2022). Cities – Commuters:

https://www.newindianexpress.com/cities/hyderabad/2018/may/05/hyderabad-commuters-spend-three-minutes-per-km-1810315.html#:~:text=Hyderabad%20commuters%20spend%20three%20minutes%20per%20km%20A,%7C%20A%2B%20A%20A-%20By%20Express%20News%20Service

Statistics.Com (2022). Population Maps India. New Delhi.

https://www.statisticstimes.com/demographics/india/indian-states-population.php

https://www.orangenews9.com

https://orangenews9.com/annual-floods-natural-disasters-or-manmade/:

www.dissentmagazine.org

https://www.dissentmagazine.org/article/india-economic-development-and-political-stability-in-india

www.mapsofindia.com

https://www.mapsofindia.com/maps/india/seismiczone.htm

Made in United States
North Haven, CT
30 September 2022

24806848R00071